PROFESSIONAL PROPOSAL WRITING

Professional Proposal Writing

Jane Fraser

Gower

Published by
Gower Publishing Limited
Gower House
Croft Road
Aldershot
Hampshire GU11 3HR
England

Gower
Old Post Road
Brookfield
Vermont 05036
USA

Jane Fraser has asserted her right under the Copyright, Designs and Patents Act 1988 to be identified as the author of this work.

British Library Cataloguing in Publication Data
Fraser, Jane
 Professional Proposal Writing
 I. Title
808.066658

ISBN 0–566–07536-9

        Library of Congress Cataloging–in–Publication Data
Fraser, Jane, 1954–
    Professional proposal writing/Jane Fraser.
       p.   cm.
    Includes index.
    ISBN 0–566–07536–9
    1. Proposal writing in business.   I. Title
    HF5718.5.F73   1995
    658. 15'224—dc20
                                                                95–13042
                                                                     CIP
Typeset in Palatino by Poole Typesetting (Wessex) Ltd, Bournemouth and printed in Great Britain by Biddles Limited, Guildford

Contents

Figures

Preface

How did this book come to be written – and why should I be the one to write it? The story started a few years ago, when I was working as Editorial Director in an international communications agency, specializing in producing technical and marketing publications for the healthcare industry. Proposal writing was an important part of my job. Yet, despite my background as a professional technical writer, it was a challenge for which I was initially poorly equipped. What was the best way to structure a proposal? What style should it be written in? How could we demonstrate our capabilities to our clients in writing? How could we differentiate ourselves from the competition? What qualities distinguished a winning proposal?

To my surprise there were no ready-made answers to these questions. I looked in vain for the definitive handbook on proposal writing – in fact, I found that hardly anything had been published on the topic. So, like so many others before me, I learned on the job. I was grateful for the kind advice of colleagues who had been this way before me, and who had learned by bitter experience what does and does not work. Before long I was offering proposal writing advice to others, but still there was no simple how-to handbook to which I could refer them.

Later, when I established my own company to train people in business and technical writing skills, I found that proposal writing was one of the topics most often requested. Through the Continuing Professional Development Centre at the University of Oxford, I was asked to teach proposal writing to a wide range of businesses – from actuaries to engineers. I began to learn about the proposal writing problems faced by small entrepreneurial companies and large international organizations. I became aware of the challenges posed by competitive pitching to traditional professions such as accountancy and the law. Then I realized – it was time to write the book for which I had been searching all along.

Professional Proposal Writing is not an academic textbook. It is a practical handbook based on personal experience, plus the generous contributions of dozens of colleagues and course participants. It draws on many disciplines, from marketing to copywriting. It is intended to be read, discussed, argued with – but, above all, *used*. It cannot provide the answer to every question, but it can provide a firm foundation on which to build proposal-writing strategies that are right for *your* company. I hope it will play a small part in the success of your business in years to come.

Jane Fraser

Acknowledgements

My thanks to all the clients, course participants and friends who contributed to the writing of this book, especially Keith Austin, Kathleen Carey, Jan Field, Jenny Holman, Sally Kelly, The Medicine Group, Maggie Pettifer, Diane Storey and Richard Tomlinson. Thanks also to Anna Morris and Peter Combey of the Continuing Professional Development Centre at the University of Oxford, which provided the platform for the courses on which this book is based.

Jane Fraser

1 Introduction

Let's start this book with a basic question – what do we mean by 'a proposal'? This book is about proposals written by one company to persuade another, the client, to buy tailormade services or products. For convenience I've called these documents 'project proposals'. For example, a proposal might be written to persuade the client that your company is the best choice to run a conference, install a new software system, or build a new bridge.

Proposals are an increasingly common fact of life for all sorts of companies. In some industries, such as advertising, the proposal has always played an important part in gaining new business. In other sectors, the competitive proposal is a relatively new phenomenon, often arriving in the wake of new public sector regulations on 'compulsory competitive tendering' or 'market testing'.

Depending on your industry you might be in the habit of referring to 'pitches' rather than proposals. You may also talk about 'tenders' or 'quotes' – terms which often cover more than simply a price quotation. You may be in a profession such as accountancy where 'beauty parades' are becoming a common means of persuading clients to retain you on a long-term basis. The principles discussed in this book apply to all these situations.

Proposals and *your* company

If you are reading this book, you're probably already well aware of how important written proposals are to your company. For any firm providing a tailormade service or product, or for any professional consulting organization, proposals are likely to play an essential role in winning new business.

Whatever business you're in, from the brash world of direct marketing to the more restrained environment of professional services, there is no getting away from the fact that *the proposal is written to sell*. Whether you're a metallurgist or a managing director, if you're writing a proposal, you're selling. You may be selling something tangible, or something intangible – an idea, a point of view, a method of doing things, even a person. Although you, the proposal writer, may not consider yourself a 'salesperson', that is the job you are doing when you sit down to write a proposal.

That doesn't mean that your approach should consist of a brash 'hard sell'. That's rarely the right path to follow. What *is* appropriate is a moderate, gentle reasoned approach which is nevertheless highly persuasive. It is possible to remain dignified and professional, and retain your integrity, while also selling your services as hard as you can.

This book concentrates mainly on proposals to sell to an external client, but proposals can also be used as internal documents to persuade senior management, or other parts of your organization, to take a particular course of action. The same principles can also be applied to internal proposals, as well as to such documents as grant applications and submissions to government and other institutions. Although you might not be 'selling' in the usual sense of the word, you will be using very similar techniques to persuade your readers that what you are proposing is the right – indeed the only – course of action.

The power of a well-written proposal

Clients often make important buying decisions largely on the strength of the proposal. Your company's proposal will usually have to stand up to tough comparison with those of your competitors. In today's ultra-competitive market, a well-written proposal can make the difference between gaining or losing a contract.

So, it makes sense to ensure that your proposals are planned, organized and written to make the most of the sales opportunity the proposal offers. To succeed in business you need good ideas, but ideas alone are not enough. You have to convince your customers that you possess the competence, commitment and creativity to make your ideas happen. You need to be able to paint a picture of your organization and what you can do for your client. You must show your client exactly why they should choose you rather than your competitors.

Whether you're in market research or management consultancy, software or sales training, the proposal provides an invaluable means of showing what you will do, how well you will do it, and why you will do it better than anyone else. All this can be accomplished in a professional and dignified manner, through the strength of your arguments, the clarity with which they are expressed, and the concern for the customer that shines through in everything you write.

When customers have to make a choice between several proposals, there will often be little objective difference between what is proposed, or the cost of the project. This is where more subtle factors come into play. If the customer has to work hard to understand what is being proposed, because of poor organization, then your company loses ground. If the customer is confused by imprecise language, your credibility slips. If the customer is annoyed by wordiness, redundancy or irrelevance in the proposal, you may be about to lose the contract.

If, on the other hand, your ideas and arguments are presented in a logical sequence, you will carry your reader with you. If your analysis makes the customer feel that they are dealing with people who understand the problem and are confident of the solution, you're halfway to gaining their agreement. If you speak the same language, and show you share the customer's preoccupations and aspirations, they will look forward to working with you.

The proposal that conveys its key messages quickly, clearly and convincingly has a head start against the competition. By contrast, the penalties of the ill-thought-out, sloppily written proposal are clear. Bad proposals lose business. You may feel that your good professional and personal relationship with the customer puts you in a privileged position, but can you be sure? Once a proposal is submitted it represents the quality standards set by your organization. A sketchy or sloppy proposal may lead to your being turned down by people you have never even met.

How this book can help you win new business

If you find proposal writing a depressing or daunting task, you're not alone. For many people proposal writing comes as an unwelcome interruption to their 'real' jobs. Whether you are a manager or a technical expert, a sales professional or a consultant, putting your ideas down on paper may seem a difficult and unrewarding chore, even though you know that no proposal means no business.

You may be one of the many people who are confident and polished speakers, but uncomfortable when addressing an unseen audience. You may be afraid of making embarrassing mistakes in grammar or spelling. You may be frustrated by the demands proposal writing makes on your time. You may simply feel you need help.

Help is at hand. *Effective proposal writing is a skill that can be learned.* There's no mystique. If you are a professional in business, you can be a professional on paper. If you can think logically and speak your native language, you can communicate your ideas. If you know your business and your customers, you can write a proposal that works. It's certainly not necessary to have a special gift for writing – good business writers are made, not born.

Proposal writing is an everyday skill like cooking a meal. You follow a recipe which will give you acceptable results every time. Naturally you can add or subtract ingredients to suit the tastes of your readers. If you do it well, your readers will come back for more!

This is a recipe book. It aims to help people in any kind of business write the kind of proposal that wins contracts. The practical tips and techniques it contains will help you produce proposals that are:

- clear
- concise
- well-organized
- accurate
- error-free
- lively and interesting
- pleasant to read
- reader-focused
- persuasive
- authoritative

The guidelines in this book will help you to write more confidently and more quickly, but most of all they will help give you the competitive edge you need to succeed.

Writing a good proposal is a sales task, not a literary challenge. You do not need to have perfect grammar or spelling, or to have been top of your class in English composition. True, minor mistakes in English can be irritating to your client and you should make every effort to eradicate them. Usually this is easily done by asking someone else to help you check for mistakes once the proposal is written.

As a proposal writer your first job is not to dot the 'i's and cross the 't's. It is to write the proposal in a way that is easily understood and gets across your key selling messages. This is not a mysterious process – there are rules that you can follow. The next chapters will tell you how to do it.

Proposal preparation
Chapter 2 describes the essential preparatory work that must be done before you sit down to write your proposal. In particular it examines the marketing decisions that must be made.

Structuring your proposal

To understand what you are proposing, clients first have to be able to find their way around the proposal. Chapter 3 describes the standard sections that are included in most proposals, and some variations on the standard structure.

Thinking and writing logically

A logical structure is kind to your client and creates a professional image. Chapter 4 shows you some techniques for ordering your material logically within the main sections of your proposal, and how you can use headings and other devices to guide your reader through the proposal.

Client-friendly writing

Writing to suit your client is all part of providing excellent customer service. Chapter 5 sets out some ground rules of reader psychology that will help you to structure and write your proposal in a way that demands the least possible effort from the reader.

Clear writing

A clearly written proposal conveys your ideas effectively and makes your client feel respected and cared for. Chapter 6 shows you how to write simply and concisely, making your proposal easy to read and understand.

Powerful writing

Chapter 7 teaches you some skills that are normally practised only by professional copywriters – highly effective techniques that will help you to sell your ideas with every word you write.

Selling the people and the company

Chapter 8 looks at what, for many companies, is the most crucial part of the proposal – the part that tells you about the people who will be working on the project, and about your company's track record. This chapter will give you some specific techniques for ensuring that you sell yourselves in the most polished and professional way.

Selling with the summary
More people will read the summary than any other part of your proposal. Chapter 9 shows you how to make sure that your summary sells as well as encapsulates all the necessary information.

The well-groomed proposal
Minor errors can be irritating to your clients and detract from the professional image of your company. Chapter 10 describes some quick, simple and effective ways of polishing your proposal.

Keeping up appearances
The right physical format can make a significant contribution to the success of your proposal. Chapter 11 shows you how to make your proposal look smart without spending too much time or money.

Checking your proposal
Chapter 12 provides handy checklists you can use to make sure that your proposal is fit to print.

The covering letter
A good covering letter can make your proposal stand out from the competition and enhance its chances of acceptance. Chapter 13 describes a simple seven-point plan for writing a snappy, sales-oriented covering letter.

Presenting your proposal
You will often be asked to present your proposal in person. Chapter 14 tells you all you need to know about preparing your 'script' and visual aids.

Learning from experience
Chapter 15 shows how you can learn from both successful and unsuccessful proposals, sharing the information throughout your organization and continuously improving your proposal-writing expertise.

This book recognizes that your time is precious. Therefore it does not ask you to do 'exercises' that you won't have time for. However it does give you *Action Points* at the end of every chapter. These suggest steps you can take, right now, to improve the quality of your proposals and increase your success in winning new business.

So, please use this book in the way that suits you best, to help you write winning proposals, quickly and efficiently. Read it at one go if that suits you, or dip into it as you need to. It's your proposal and it's your business – the aim of this book is to help you make both as successful as possible.

2 Proposal preparation

This chapter covers everything you need to do *before* you put pen to paper or finger to keyboard. It's pointless to start writing your proposal until you have been through these vital steps, just as you cannot build a house until you have laid the foundations.

As with real-life foundation-digging, proposal groundwork can be tiring, messy and time-consuming – but it is necessary. Careful planning and research at this stage will avoid wasted effort and will make the process of writing the proposal smoother and faster.

There are seven steps to effective proposal preparation.

1   Identify the client's needs.
2   Do your background research.
3   Decide what you are going to propose.
4   Clarify your marketing strategy.
5   List your proposal objectives.
6   Assign roles and brief the proposal team.
7   Draw up a schedule for writing, revising and final production.

Let's go through these steps one by one.

Identify the client's needs

As any salesperson will tell you the client's perception of their own needs is crucial to successful selling. Whatever you are trying to sell, it must fill a need. You can't sell someone something they don't need. Or, to be more precise, you can't sell someone something they don't *think* or *feel* they need.

Often the need will be obvious, but sometimes it will be hidden. You can discover or develop needs, but you can never invent them.

If your proposal is to be successful, it must demonstrate that there is a need and that you understand it completely. Only then can you convince the client of the value of your solution. Before you start to write your proposal you must identify your client's needs, break them down into small sections and look at them from every angle.

Where are you starting from?

Different proposals have different starting points. You might be devising the proposal in response to a client's request, after an encouraging preliminary meeting. You might be responding to an impersonal published 'invitation to tender' from a public sector body. You might be putting forward your ideas 'on spec' to a client who you think might be interested. You will probably be in competition with other companies, but it's conceivable that you might be the only company proposing.

The client will often begin the process by stating a specific need, but this may not be the full story. The client's statement of their need may be incomplete or poorly defined. There may be other more subtle needs which it will pay you to seek out. Occasionally you may find that the need the client has highlighted is not the 'real' need and you will be faced with the task of persuading and educating them about their needs.

Sometimes, the client may already have analysed their own needs and decided exactly what should be done, but remains to be persuaded that your organization can do it, at the right price. This is often the situation when local authorities, government departments or large companies call for competitive tenders.

Often, the client will have a clear idea of their end goal, but very little idea of the best way of achieving it. They will be hoping that by asking several companies to propose different solutions to their problems, they will find the best and most economic solution.

Occasionally the client may already have decided that you are the best firm for the job but wants your ideas on how to go about it. This puts you in an enviable position, but you still have the task of convincing the customer that your plan is good and worth the money they will be spending on it.

Get a brief – or write your own

Before asking you to propose the client will usually have some idea of what they want to achieve. Typically, you or one of your colleagues will have attended a preliminary meeting at which the client's needs (however vaguely defined) were discussed. You will have been invited to submit a proposal based on the premise that your company might be able to fulfil those needs. In other words, you will have been given a brief.

The quality and detail of briefs can vary widely, depending on the client and the industry, from a large bound volume to a throw-away line in conversation. If the need has been very specifically defined by the client, the brief may be quite detailed and probably written down. This is usually the case with local authority and government tenders, and often with large companies:

> 'Landscape consultants are invited to submit plans and costs for an adventure playground on the site of the former Victoria Glueworks. It must be suitable for children under 12 years and include the following components … '

The ultimate in detailed briefs are the tender forms often used in the engineering and building industries, where the proposer simply has to answer a long list of highly specific questions and enter prices and time estimates on a detailed specification, which may be many pages long. Such tenders offer minimal scope for needs analysis, or indeed for any of the techniques described in this book – except for the covering letter, which then becomes an important selling tool (see Chapter 13).

In many industries, however, the need will be less well defined and the brief less specific. A motor manufacturer: 'We want to make this the most exciting car launch ever'. A pharmaceutical company: 'We want an incentive programme that will really encourage the reps'. A mail-order company: 'We want someone to improve our computerized system for order processing'.

If the invitation to pitch comes 'out of the blue' or after only a very sketchy initial meeting, you will probably want to arrange one or more briefing meetings at which you and the client can work together to identify their needs. Depending on what you are being asked to do, you may want to visit the client's offices or factory and talk to a whole range of people in order to get a complete picture of what they are trying to achieve.

The client will usually see the sense of this. The time they invest in meeting you will be well repaid in the quality of your proposal. You are only likely to be refused a meeting point blank when a very large number of firms are being asked to propose and the client does not have the time to meet them all. In that case they may decide that it is unfair to give any one firm an advantage by agreeing to a meeting.

In the absence of a clear brief you will be using information gained by hook or by crook in order to write your own brief. Before visiting the client's site, or inviting them to your office for a briefing meeting, make a note of all the things you need to know before you can begin to understand their needs.

For example, before you even begin to think of proposing a computerized order-processing system for the mail-order company, you will probably want to clarify what 'a better system' means to them:

- Do they want a system that is easier for them to use?
- Do they want a system that allows them to bill their customers more quickly?
- Do they want a system that is more reliable?
- Do they want a system that allows quicker delivery?
- Do they want to have 'the latest' system, or 'what the competition uses'?

In addition, you will want factual information about:

- the company's existing computer hardware and software
- their business in general
- their 'mission' and goals
- their budget for this project
- related projects they have already commissioned, or plan to commission.

It will also pay you to enquire into other, more subjective, aspects of their need, such as:

- the client's own ideas on how their problems might be solved
- the attitude of the staff towards the current technology and the prospect of new introductions
- the company's past experience with computer consultants
- the kind of working relationship they would like with a new supplier – ask them to describe their 'ideal' supplier.

Only when you have the answers to these questions will you be able to 'write your own brief' for the proposal.

If the project is large and complex, and the client has not provided a written brief, it is useful to ring the client and briefly outline your own interpretation of what they're asking you to propose, so they can confirm you're on the right track. Done in the right way, checking out the brief can be a way of demonstrating commitment to winning the contract – it doesn't have to be an indication of weakness.

Do your background research

Different proposals will involve different amounts of research. We've already talked about research to identify the client's needs. Research will almost certainly be necessary to provide the solutions and recommendations that form the body of the proposal.

Occasionally this research may be so extensive that you can and should negotiate a fee for preparing the proposal. The research produces information that is valuable in its own right. For example, you might have to commission some market research to support your proposal. This may be valuable to the client even if they do not eventually award you the contract, so it is reasonable to check if they are willing to pay for it. If they refuse you will have to decide whether the competitive advantage the research gives you in preparing your proposal is worth the time, effort and expense incurred.

Likewise, proposals in management consultancy often divide the work into two phases – a diagnostic phase in which the consultant investigates the client's needs and produces a report suggesting solutions, and an implementation phase in which the chosen solutions are introduced into the client company. The client will be expected to pay for both phases. The proposal might say broadly how you would go about the diagnostic phase, but would be careful to avoid giving away too much 'free consultancy'.

On the other hand, it can work to your advantage if the proposal tells the client one or two things they did not know and will find useful. You needn't give much away, but the little nuggets you do provide will be seen as proving an exceptional service.

Keep a proposal database

Don't neglect the wealth of material you almost certainly have hidden away in your company files. Past proposals and the accompanying research will provide you with valuable information and ideas. Never throw away old proposals, even those that were unsuccessful. Keep a proposal database available to everyone involved in writing proposals. If you use a word-processor, keep standard proposal elements such as your charging structure and the CVs of key staff on disk. These 'proposal templates' can be dropped into proposals as they stand, or modified to suit the current project.

Incidentally, if you do keep a database of standard proposal elements, remember to eradicate any company names from the sections you plan to 'drop in'. Someone I know (all right, it was me) once 'recycled' a proposal for Smith and Bloggs and sent it to Jones and Sproggit. Unfortunately, I had not been scrupulously careful in checking the word-processed document. Jones and

Sproggit accepted the proposal, but wrote a charming letter to say that they 'particularly appreciated the suggestion that our competitors Smith and Bloggs should provide lunch in the boardroom during the training course'. I was grateful for their good humour and have never made the same mistake again.

Get to know your client

To devise an appropriate marketing strategy, and to write an effective proposal, you need to know as much as possible about the people who will read your proposal, who will be making the final decision, and whose opinions will influence that decision. Most proposals will be read by more than one person. Sometimes it is easy to find out who your readers are, sometimes you may have to make an educated guess. But time spent thinking about your readers – in other words, your customers – is always worthwhile.

The company

If you are lucky you will have already met some of the people from your client company and know quite a bit about them. Often you may have to do some background research. Knowing about the environment in which your client operates will help you to find the best solution to their needs. It will also allow you to project an image of confidence and professionalism and might help to protect you against 'shooting yourself in the foot' with an inappropriate remark.

You will want to know as much as you can about their business, for example:

- what they do
- who their customers are
- who their competitors are
- the culture of the industry and of the company.

Research into the company itself is relatively easy. Sources of information include:

- annual reports
- company brochures

- mission statement
- advertisements
- industry/trade associations
- articles in the national, local, financial or trade press – it's a good idea to keep a cuttings file on all your past, present and potential clients
- online business databases, e.g. Dun and Bradstreet.

The people

Research into individuals is a little harder than research into companies. In an ideal world, you would like to know:

- who is going to read the report, their responsibilities and position
- who are the decision-makers
- who are the 'gatekeepers' who can allow you to get to the decision-makers
- who are the influencers
- are there any 'blockers' who have reason to see that your proposal is rejected?

You can usually put these questions discreetly to whoever is your closest client contact without causing offence. If you are told that decisions are reached by consensus, you will have to be sensitive to 'vibes'. Does the enthusiastic young executive who invited you to propose have the final say, or is he or she likely to be overruled by the MD? Is it all down to the purchasing department in the end, whatever the recommendations of the other departments? If the head of human resources is the formal chair of the review panel, does he or she really just agree with whatever the training manager decides? You will need all your interpersonal skills to unravel these sensitive issues.

Delving even deeper into your client's corporate and individual personalities, you want to know:

- *Their personal objectives*   In addition to their stated objectives, it is highly likely that individuals will have some personal bees in their bonnets. They may be happy to admit to some of these: 'I've always felt that our company should be more involved in environmental issues'. Other objectives may be very private. Clients rarely say 'I need to make a big success of this launch to win my next promotion', but you can be sure that many will be thinking it. Be alert to any signals about these personal objectives.

- *Their knowledge of the subject* Some of your readers may be fascinated by the technical detail, others may know little and care less. Depending on who are the key buyers or influencers, you may decide to deal with the technical detail in your proposal in different ways.
- *Their buying criteria* Different companies, and different individuals, may be preoccupied by:
  - quality
  - speed
  - novelty
  - credibility
  - price.

  Don't be afraid to ask clients politely: 'What will make you choose one proposal above the others?' Often they will tell you. If the answer is evasive or confused, you may have to look for clues in their conversation, or in the brief itself.
- *Their prejudices* People may already have a fixed idea of the 'right' way of doing things. They may have pet loves and hates: 'We've always prided ourselves on being classier than the competition'. 'The MD thinks management training's a waste of time'. It will do no harm to subtly acknowledge these prejudices in the way you write your proposal. Even if you decide to propose something that runs counter to the client's prejudices, if you know what they are, you will be able to marshal your arguments against them.

Check out the competition

The more you know about your competitors the easier it will be to ensure that your ideas are different and/or better. Some clients may be quite forthcoming about who is pitching for the job and may even be willing to discuss their opinions of the strengths and weaknesses of your competitors.

It does no harm to ask who your competitors are. If you can find out, you can do the same kind of research into them as you would into your client company. Depending on the nature of your business you may be able to examine samples of their work or talk (discreetly) to past clients. It's useful to keep a 'competitors' file so that you can re-use the information you gather.

Decide what you are going to propose

Having analysed and identified the client's needs, you will probably already have quite a few ideas on how you are going to meet them. You may find that you have a range of options open to you, all of which have their advantages and disadvantages. Which options are you going to choose? What ideas are you going to suggest?

Look for the most saleable solution

Your final proposal will depend not only on what works, but on what is most attractive to the client. In other words, there will be marketing as well as technical considerations.

You will be looking for a solution that:

- works – i.e. meets the client's true needs. This is the number one consideration
- fits the brief (but see below for going beyond the brief)
- meets the client's subjective as well as objective requirements
- will make a healthy profit for your company
- can be achieved within any constraints the client has set (e.g. time, budget)
- can beat the competition.

Unless you are a one-person business, the decision on what to propose will usually be made by a team. Depending on the style of your business, the decision-making process could consist of anything from a brainstorming session to a complex process of research and reporting.

Decide whether you should deviate from the brief

If the client has given you a detailed brief, when should you go beyond it? Should you include solutions to problems they don't even know they have? Should you argue with their own interpretation of their needs? The decision to go beyond the brief is essentially a marketing decision. Do the benefits of surprising the client outweigh the risks?

There's no simple answer to these questions – it depends on the individual client.

The receptive client

When proposing for the private sector, you will often have plenty of leeway to re-examine and redefine the need. It will usually pay you to examine the client's needs from 'first principles' rather than just assuming that their own analysis is complete. They may have missed a vital point or you may have some good ideas about other ways in which they could make good use of your services.

A successful consultancy should analyse the needs of the client and come up with new ways of meeting them. This can be good for the client – your new idea may be better, or cheaper, or both. It can be good for you, if a new idea gives you your unique selling point – you may be able to isolate some aspect of the need which no-one but you can fill.

If you have a great idea, go for it! But be careful, this can be quite a tricky area. Theoretically, good business people are always ready to listen to new ideas, but they may need a little coaxing. You may be challenging the client's preconceived notions – it's only human nature to feel attached to something you have spent a lot of time thinking about. Never challenge them aggressively. Instead try to demonstrate that you understand their problems and offer constructive solutions for discussion.

Deviating from the brief — a case history

Let's take a real-life example of a consultancy who specialized in environmental quality standards. Their client said:

> 'We need someone to help our open-cast mining company meet the requirements of the BS5750 Quality Management System.'

The consultancy, because of their special knowledge and expertise, realized that, in a few years time, the same company would also need to meet the new standard for environmental management, BS7750 – and later, European quality standards. In the very long term, the client might not be able to stay in business unless these standards were met.

The consultancy saw scope for both needs – the immediate need for BS5750 and the future need for BS7750 – to be addressed simultaneously. This would have advantages for both parties. The client would be able to reach the new standards sooner and at a lower overall cost. And the consultancy, as perhaps the only company that could complete both services simultaneously, would have a unique advantage over the competition.

So they redefined the need as:

'We need someone to help us meet the requirements for both the BS5750 Quality Management System and the BS7750 Environmental Management System.'

In doing this, they were aware of the potential pitfalls. They asked themselves what would happen if the client:

- had never heard of BS7750 and didn't see why they should have it
- had heard of BS7750 but had already decided they couldn't afford to pay for both projects at the same time
- was fully committed to BS7750 and had already asked another company for a proposal to help them obtain it.

They concluded that if they were to win the contract they would have to re-educate the client, telling them all about BS7750 and why they needed it, and especially why they should aim to have it sooner rather than later. They knew that they had to make a convincing argument for spending a little more money now, to save money later. They knew they had to work hard to persuade the client of the time and cost advantages of using one company to perform both tasks. They succeeded, by recognizing that they were going to surprise the client and preparing them carefully for the 'shock of the new'.

To summarize, if you go beyond the brief, you will have to have a good reason, and be able to explain it. Clients may find it insulting if you imply that your ideas are 'better' than theirs. If you are putting forward suggestions outside the brief, you will need to make sure that the client is educated into a receptive frame of mind. You can do this through a detailed explanation of your reasoning.

If in doubt, check it out

If possible check out the acceptability of additions to the brief with an informal 'phone call. This may save you time and trouble if the client is not willing to consider additional ideas or doesn't agree with your analysis of the problem.

The inflexible brief

If you have been supplied with a minutely detailed brief, or even a form to complete, check carefully whether variations are acceptable. Your proposal is likely to go through a formal scoring system which may not be able to cope with deviations from the brief. You do not want to be marked down or even thrown out for simply failing to follow the rules.

Some clients will allow you to submit a so-called 'variant solution'. In other words you submit two proposals, one of which follows the brief, and another which doesn't.

A dramatic example of what can go wrong if you surprise the public sector with an unexpected 'good' idea is provided by the controversy in June 1993 over the decision to award an important naval contract to the Devonport rather than the Rosyth dockyard. Both yards had originally submitted a similar outline proposal for building a new dock to refit Trident submarines – Devonport at £120 million and Rosyth at £130 million. Fearing that they would lose, Rosyth then came back with an alternative bid, based on reusing an existing dock, at about half the original price. The Ministry of Defence refused to even consider Rosyth's new bid, on the ostensible grounds that it failed to meet the original specification, even though this had changed repeatedly during the tendering process. Whether Rosyth were right or wrong, or whether they were the victims of political forces, is open to dispute – but they tried to buck the system and they failed.

Can you be too creative?

A final word on analysing the client's needs and devising solutions to meet them. Just occasionally, you may find that you analyse yourself out of a job. Perhaps the client needs a service that you can't or don't want to provide. Perhaps the need could be filled in a much more economical way that would mean less work for you. If you reach this point it's up to you whether you 'come clean' or go along with the client's own perception of their needs. But don't underestimate the benefits to future business of telling the client what's best for them, not for you.

Talking yourself out of a job — a case history

A true story: a company specializing in computerized engineering testing systems was asked by a washing machine manufacturer to submit a proposal for an automated testing system for the complicated wiring system inside the washing machines. Having studied the problem, the consultant went back and told the client: 'The wiring would be much easier to test if you simplified it like this. And it would work just as well.' The client's engineers were surprised, but they looked at the wiring and came back and said: 'You're right. In fact, we can make it so simple that we don't need a fancy testing system.' The consultant had talked his company out of a job. But when the next job came up, his was the company invited to quote.

Clarify your marketing strategy

A clear marketing strategy is essential, whether you're selling against competition or whether you're the sole contender. This book certainly doesn't aim to address the complexities of marketing your service or product. But it does urge you to clarify marketing matters so that you can communicate your selling message clearly to your client.

Marketing considerations will influence:

• the recommendations you make
• how you write your proposal.

Do a SWOT analysis

A standard marketing technique with which you are no doubt familiar is the SWOT (strengths, weaknesses, opportunities and threats) analysis. You can perform the SWOT analysis on a specific solution to the client's need, on your company, or on both together – the total solution.

For a mail-order processing software project, the SWOT analysis might look like Figure 2.1.

The SWOT analysis will help you decide:

- *What to propose.* If you have to make a selection between a range of different ideas that meet the need, the SWOT analysis will help you to decide which are the most saleable.
- *The strengths you will need to stress in your proposal.* This means both the strengths of your solution and the strengths of your company and its personnel. What evidence will you need to support your claims?
- *The problems you will need to address.* Should you tackle potential client concerns by answering them up front? For example, if you are small, you may need to give case histories to show that you can still deliver on time and on budget. Weaknesses can sometimes be presented as strengths. 'Small' may be seen as indicating a lack of resources. But it can also mean personal attention, plus low overheads and therefore a reasonable price.
- *The competitive arguments you will have to counter.* It's rarely appropriate to attack the competition directly, but you can sow the seeds of doubt in the client's mind by subtly undermining your competitors' likely arguments.

It's vitally important to realize that the SWOT analysis varies with the situation. What is regarded as a strength by one client may be seen as a weakness by another. You cannot do a generic SWOT analysis on your service or on your company which relates to all clients and all projects. For example, the fact that you are a large, market-leading company might seem like a strength when you are selling to another large company. But it might be considered a weakness if you are selling to a small local

STRENGTHS	WEAKNESSES
• We've already completed one system similar to this • We've completed other projects for mail–order businesses • We have the capacity to start next week • We can provide glowing references from past customers	• We've never worked for this customer before • We're small, so they might think we don't have the capacity • We're based 200 miles away from the customer – they might perceive this as a problem
OPPORTUNITIES	THREATS
• If we win this project, there will probably be work for other companies in this mail–order group • Winning this project will give us experience we can use on other projects • Even if we don't win this project, a good proposal might help us win future work	• An off-the-shelf order-processing system has just come onto the market • Zap software are probably competing, and they are a bigger and better-known firm • The brief's very vague – we could propose something bigger and more expensive than they want

Figure 2.1   Example of SWOT analysis

firm with a limited budget who might assume that your services would be out of their league.

Identify your key competitive advantages

To beat the competition you must emphasize those aspects of your solution or service that make you better than your competitors. You will be able to select these from the Strengths section of your SWOT analysis.

Your proposal can and should mention all your strengths, but should highlight those that give you a competitive advantage. It is unrealistic to expect all your strengths to differentiate you from your competitors. For example, you may be competing with other companies with similarly broad experience, convenient location, and so on. Under these circumstances you might decide to highlight the creative nature of your solution or the depth of knowledge and outstanding track record of your project team.

You may be able to identify a unique selling point (USP) – one key factor that gives you the edge. Or there may be a group of small advantages which, taken together, differentiate you from the competition and make an unassailable case for choosing your proposal.

Note that your key competitive advantages will not be the same for every proposal. They will vary with the client, the project and the competition.

Some typical key competitive advantages might be:

- We have a unique solution to your problem.
- We have exceptional experience with this type of project.
- We have unique access to key experts in the field.
- Our large size gives us the capability to handle this large and complex project.
- Our small size means that your project receives personal attention from our most experienced staff.
- We will devise a tailormade solution which will never be offered to anyone else.
- We have access to a ready-made solution which will save you money.

The first advantage is probably the most compelling. If you have a way of filling the client's needs that no-one else will have thought of, that's great. But beware – few ideas are so remarkable that you can guarantee none of your competitors will have had the same brainwave. In that case you may have to look for other advantages.

Note that some of the suggestions above are contradictory. You have to make the most of your qualities to distinguish yourself from the competition as clearly and credibly as possible.

List your proposal objectives

Once you have done your research, got to know your client, analysed the client's needs, come up with ways of meeting them, and decided on your marketing strategy, you are ready to start writing your proposal. At this stage it is worthwhile spending a few minutes writing a list of your proposal objectives. If the objectives are clearly set out everyone involved in writing the proposal will know exactly what they are trying to achieve.

Your key objective will usually be obvious – you want the customer to buy your service or product, preferably at the asking price. Write this down, in one sentence.

> Persuade Smith and Jones Ltd to buy our custom-designed order-processing software.

> Convince Powerdex plc that we are the best choice to provide management consultancy services to help them find partners in Eastern Europe.

> Persuade Leviathan Insurance to let us organize their annual sales conference.

Then you can start breaking down your objective into several sub-objectives. Typical objectives for any proposal would be to persuade the client that:

- you understand their needs
- you have an effective way of fulfilling their needs
- your recommendations are the *best* way of fulfilling their needs

- your organization is the one best equipped to fulfil their needs
- your price for fulfilling their needs is justified.

So the proposal for the mail-order company with the overall objective to 'Persuade Smith and Jones Ltd to buy our custom-designed order-processing software' might break down into these sub-objectives:

Persuade Smith and Jones that:

- custom-designed software will enable them to process more orders with fewer staff, deliver orders faster, and bill customers earlier
- off-the-shelf packages are inadequate for their needs
- a custom-designed system will eventually save money by making them more efficient
- we have unique experience in this area that sets us apart from the competition
- because we are experts we can design a system that will not only work, but will be easy for people to use
- we have the capacity to develop, install and test the system before their deadline
- we can provide reliable long-term maintenance and support
- we can do all this at a price they can afford.

As you clarify your proposal objectives, you will begin to think about the facts and arguments that you will need to support each point, and about which sections of the proposal they will go into. The list of proposal objectives will also highlight areas that may need further research. For example, if an off-the shelf package is available, what are its strengths and weaknesses? If your company has carried out similar projects, what exactly was involved? Can you draw any parallels that will help to convince your new client that the project will work?

Assign roles and brief the proposal team

Most proposals are a team effort. They may be written by one person, who obtains the input of others, or they may be divided into sections, each of which will be the responsibility of a different individual or department. However, it is important for one person to have an overview of the proposal and to take the ultimate responsibility for commissioning and co-ordinating the work of others. It will be up to this proposal 'leader' to ensure that the proposal meets its objectives and that it is delivered to the client on time.

It's important to decide at the outset who is going to be responsible for what, and to agree on deadlines. This saves time, confusion and potential disaster. Typical tasks to be allocated include:

- writing different sections
- obtaining quotes and estimates from different departments or external suppliers
- internal approval (e.g. do all proposals need the approval of the MD or the legal department?)
- final editing and checking of the finished proposal
- typing, printing, binding and photocopying.

It may sometimes be appropriate for a representative of the client company to become part of the proposal writing team. For example, a proposal to be submitted to the board of a big company may have been through one or more drafts, which have been modified on the advice of an executive at a lower level.

Draw up a schedule for writing, revising and final production

The client will probably ask for proposals to reach them by a certain date. Draw up a schedule for preparing your proposal to meet that deadline. If possible, include three or four days at the end to allow for disasters.

Be realistic about the length of time it will take you to write the proposal. One way of estimating writing time (not including planning time) is to take the expected length of the proposal (see 'Setting a page budget', p. 68), and express it in terms of numbers of words. A page of one-and-a-half line spaced text is about 350 words.

How much can each person realistically write in a day? Think about the last report or proposal you wrote. How long did it take you? Most people, *if they are doing nothing else*, will be able to generate no more than 2,000 words of carefully considered prose in a day. Proposal writers will probably have other calls on their time, so even 1,000 words a day might be quite an optimistic estimate. Be conservative in your estimates and delegate *early* if you foresee problems.

Know your own working style. If you are one of those people who do their best work the night before it's needed, set yourself a deadline that will allow other people to complete *their* part in a reasonable time, rather than waiting around for you and then having to work in an unreasonable hurry.

Remember that once the first draft of the proposal is completed, you will need to allow time for it to be read by other members of the proposal team and possibly by senior management or the legal department. You will also need to allow time for final editing and checking, printing, photocopying, binding etc. All these steps are described in Chapters 10–12.

It goes almost without saying that a proposal should *never* be late. It is often the first impression a client will get of the level of customer service to be expected from your organization, so don't fall at the first hurdle. If you can deliver your proposal to the client a couple of days before it's expected, you will have given them a pleasant surprise and created a good image for your company.

If the client has not set a deadline but has asked for proposals 'as soon as possible', you will have to set your own deadline. If you do not, you run the risk of the proposal slipping to the bottom of your in-tray and festering there until things get desperate. How long you give yourself to prepare an 'as soon as possible' proposal depends on the nature of your business and the length and amount of detail required.

Summary

- **Step 1: Identify the client's needs.**

  – question the client as closely as you can
  – get a brief, or write your own

- **Step 2: Research your background.**

  – keep a proposal database
  – get to know your client
  – check out the competition
  – know the rules

- **Step 3: Decide what you are going to propose.**

  – identify the client's needs
  – look for the most saleable solution
  – decide whether you should deviate from the brief

- **Step 4: Clarify your marketing strategy.**

  – do a SWOT analysis
  – identify your key competitive advantages

- **Step 5: List your proposal objectives.**

- **Step 6: Assign roles and brief the proposal team.**

- **Step 7: Draw up a schedule for writing, revising and final production.**

Action Points

1   Examine your company or departmental system for storing old proposals. Can the proposal team gain easy access to them? Are they on disk so that sections can be dropped into current proposals? Remember to double-check that all previous client names have been taken out.

2   Look at your systems for storing information about clients and competitors. Are you having to research the same information for each new proposal? Are you relying on just one or two individuals with all the information stored in their heads?

3   Next time you write a long document, work out how many words you were able to generate in a typical day. Could you use this information to help plan your proposal deadlines better in future?

4   For your next proposal, take the time to perform a SWOT analysis. Remember to concentrate on the realities of the project in hand rather than on generic strengths and weaknesses which may not be relevant to the client in question.

3   Structuring your proposal

You have been through the steps outlined in Chapter 2 and are ready to start writing your proposal. At this stage, you will be asking yourself questions like: What sections should my proposal contain? What should go into each section? What should go in appendices, or be left out altogether? How long should it be?

Let's take a look at some common proposal formats. Proposals come in many shapes and sizes but for convenience we can divide them into two categories:

- *Comprehensive proposals* – suitable for large and complicated projects, or for introducing new clients to your organization and its capabilities. Comprehensive does not necessarily mean large; proposals should be just as long as necessary and no more (see p. 58).
- *Mini-proposals or sales letters* – sometimes a simplified proposal, or just a long letter, will do the job just as well as a more elaborate proposal. The choice of format will depend on the nature of the project and your relationship with the client. For example, the client may have asked you 'just jot something down in writing' after a sales presentation. If that's the case, a comprehensive proposal might be considered over the top. But a mini-proposal of just a few pages

would put your presentation on the record and help to clinch the sale. Similarly, you might be putting in a speculative bid for work where a full proposal might not be justified in terms of time and effort. In this case an extended letter, outlining the benefits your company could bring to the client, would be entirely appropriate.

The comprehensive proposal

When is it necessary to produce a comprehensive proposal? The answer to this question will depend on the nature of the project and the client, but here are a few good reasons for using a 'traditional' formal structure:

- the client has asked for a full or comprehensive proposal
- the client is unfamiliar with your company and its capabilities
- you do not know who is going to read your proposal
- you know that the client is a stickler for formality
- you know or suspect that your competitors will be submitting full formal proposals
- a detailed analysis of the client's need is required to support the proposal
- the proposed project is large and complex, requiring many technical details.

If you are proposing to a public sector organization, or some large companies, the proposal structure may already be laid down for you to follow. These guidelines may extend to section headings, number of pages, margins, spacing and number of copies.

There is a purpose to these rules – to allow proposals from different suppliers to be compared on equal terms, often using a formal scoring system. Some of the rules may seem petty, but you ignore them at your peril. Follow the guidelines to the letter – you want your proposal to be considered on its merits, not rejected for being written in the wrong format.

For most proposals to the private sector you will be able to choose your own structure. The one suggested below for a comprehensive proposal will probably be familiar to you and your readers. It is conventional enough to comfort the most pernick-ety of readers, yet flexible enough to give you the freedom to suit the proposal to the project. Not every project will require every section and sections can often be merged together, especially if the proposal is very short.

Remember, the purpose of the proposal is to answer all the questions that the client would like to ask you (see Figure 3.1). If you bear that in mind in the structure of your proposal you can't go wrong.

Client question	Sections that provide the answer
What's this proposal all about and how do I find my way around?	Covering letter Title page Copyright statement (if needed) *Table of contents* *Summary*
Why are you proposing?	*Introduction* *Terms of reference* *Understanding of the need*
What will you do for us?	*Recommendations* *Project plan*
How long will it take and how much will it cost?	*Schedules* *Costs*
Why choose you and not one of your competitors?	*Personnel* *Credentials*
What do I do if I like your ideas?	*The way forward*
Any other information?	*Appendices*

Figure 3.1   Structure for a comprehensive proposal

Formal/informal headings

While some proposals might use the headings listed above, you may want to adopt a less formal style and invent your own headings, with a more 'selling' flavour. For example:

> *Understanding of the need* = *The need for more effective ...*
> *Project plan*   = *Planning for success*
> *Personnel*   = *Your project team*
> *Credentials*   = *Why use ABC Associates?*

Let's consider the proposal elements in the order in which they appear (which is not necessarily the order in which you will write them).

Covering letter

See Chapter 13 for advice on how to write an effective covering letter for your proposal.

Title page

The function of the title page is to introduce the proposal to the reader. The reader should be able to see at a glance:

- what the proposal is about
- who has prepared it
- who it was prepared for
- when it was prepared.

A typical title page might look something like Figure 3.2. You might want to include other items on your title page, for example, your company logo. If your proposal is very short, you could add a mini-*Table of contents* (but keep it to 5 lines or less).

When designing your title page, think about the final presentation of your proposal. Do you want to have a cover as well as a title page? You might want the title page to be visible through a transparent cover or the title to appear in a 'window'. In Chapter 11

TERRIFIC TRAINING LTD
13 Northampton Road
Anytown
WX1 2BA
Tel: 0145 678 9111
Fax: 0145 678 9822

**Proposal for
a two–day training course
'Professional Proposal Writing'**

**Prepared for
Mr Nick Scroggins, Oxbridge Multimedia Ltd**

**by
Dr Gareth Peabody
Terrific Training Ltd**

9 December 1995

Figure 3.2   Example of title page

we will look in more detail at how to enhance the appearance of your proposal.

Copyright or confidentiality statement

Most clients treat proposals with respect. They understand that you will have worked hard on your proposal and the ideas it contains, and will give credit where it is due. Usually, if you have put forward good ideas, you will be the supplier chosen to put them into practice. However, it is not unknown for a client to show sections from one consultant's proposal to another 'pet' supplier, especially if they think they will be quoted a better price for the job by doing so.

For this reason, you may decide to make it your policy to include a copyright and/or confidentiality statement in your proposal. This is unlikely to protect you against a totally unscrupulous client who sets out deliberately to poach your ideas without paying for them. However, it may help to remind a client who might otherwise be sloppy about confidentiality to treat your intellectual property with the respect it deserves.

An appropriate statement would be:

Copyright: Terrific Training Ltd, 1995.

You can back this up with something like:

Confidential: this proposal is for internal use by Oxbridge Multimedia Ltd only, and is not to be shown or distributed to any other parties without the express permission of Terrific Training Ltd.

A straightforward copyright statement can be inserted on the title page if you wish. Any more elaborate statement regarding confidentiality is probably better tucked neatly away at the bottom of the second page, where it is visible but not too aggressive. Some people put a tiny copyright line as a footer at the bottom of each page.

© Terrific Training Ltd 1995

Table of contents

Every lengthy proposal – let's say of more than 5 pages – should include a *Table of contents*, listing the main sections and subsections of the proposal together with the page or section numbers in which they appear. The main function of the *Table of contents* is to act as a route map for the reader, enabling them to find their way around the proposal. If they want to check the costs, or refer to the CV of the principal consultant, or see how you're going to handle a specific section of the brief, they should be able to look in the *Table of contents* and go straight to the section they want.

The *Table of contents* can have another, more subtle function, however. It can act as a selling tool, underlining your key marketing messages. Scanning down the table can not only tell the reader where to find things, it can softly sell the project. This depends on using 'selling' headings and subheadings, as described in Chapter 4.

Draw up the *Table of contents* after you have finished writing the proposal. Make sure that headings and their numbers exactly match those given in the main body of the proposal. Some word-processing programs (e.g. Word and Word Perfect) have tools for creating *Tables of contents* which will help to make this task easier.

Summary

The *Summary* is one of the most important parts of the proposal. It is so important that it has a chapter all to itself (Chapter 9), where you will find all the details on how to write your *Summary* for maximum impact. Until then, here are a few key points to remember about your *Summary*:

- Most people will read the *Summary* first.
- Some important decision makers and influencers may read *only* the *Summary*.
- The function of the *Summary* is to encapsulate the reasons for the client to buy. With this in mind, it will usually include:
  – your name, company address and the title of the proposal

- a brief summary of the need you set out to meet (and the terms of reference if appropriate)
- a concise summary of how you will meet the need, stressing benefits to the client (including your ability to meet their deadlines, if relevant)
- a statement of who will carry out the project (if relevant)
- a clear statement of why the client should choose your company.
- The length of the *Summary* should be proportional to the length of the proposal. For most proposals (20 pages or less) the *Summary* should be kept to one A4 page.

Introduction

Before launching into the nuts-and-bolts of the proposal it is a good idea to introduce yourself to the client. After all, when you first meet a client, isn't that exactly what you do? You spend a few minutes saying hello and letting them know who you are before you go on to discuss their needs.

If your proposal is likely to be read by people whom you have never met and may not even have previously known of your existence, begin by stating who you are, what your company does, and perhaps give one or two outstanding examples of your work or facts about your experience. No more than that – you'll have the opportunity to go into the advantages of using your company later on in the *Credentials* section of the proposal.

A typical *Introduction* might be something like this:

This proposal has been prepared for Ashingden Health Services by Belforth Associates Ltd. Belforth Associates is a public relations consultancy specializing in the healthcare and pharmaceutical industries. Our recent experience includes public relations activities for several new hospital trusts.

After introducing yourself, you can move on to the terms of reference:

Belforth Associates has been asked to propose …

Terms of reference

Terms of reference are a necessary part of any proposal. Their function is to define exactly what you have been asked to do by the client so that everyone knows what the proposal is expected to achieve.

It is only in more formal proposals that it is essential to use the heading *Terms of reference*. In less formal proposals the *Terms of reference* are best merged with the *Introduction*. However, the statements are likely to be the same:

- who asked you to propose (give the name of the person or the department if appropriate, as well as the company name)
- in general, what they asked you to propose
- any constraints of time, budget, location etc. that were mentioned at the outset
- any additions you may have found it necessary to make to the *Terms of reference*.

Examples

Belforth Associates has been asked to propose a programme of public relations activities to establish an appropriate image for the Trust both among health professionals and the general public in the Ashingden area.

Or for a much more specific brief:

Mr W Snodgrass, Operations Director, GBH Engineering, has asked Caterall Food Services to put forward a proposal for the catering contract at the Smithfield site for the period January 1995–January 1996. Caterall Food Services understand the terms of reference to be as follows:

- Hot food must be available in the canteen for a maximum of 550 employees at these times: 7.30 – 9.00 and 12.00 – 14.00.
- Hot and cold drinks and light snacks must also be available at five specified locations at all times between 8.00 and 18.00.
- No additional catering staff posts will be created.

- A minimum cost saving of 10% (compared with current levels) is required.
- In addition, Caterall Food Services have assumed that existing canteen facilities and catering equipment must be used where feasible, with refurbishment where necessary.

Understanding of the need

This section – sometimes referred to by clients as the 'understanding of the requirement' or 'needs analysis' – provides the rationale for the project proposal. In other words, it tells the client why they need the services you propose to provide. To do this you will need to show the client that you:

- understand their business
- understand and empathize with their problems
- are listening to their own analysis of their needs
- have further analysed their needs to provide a rational basis for your recommendations.

Obviously the relative importance of these various functions will change with the nature of the project. In some cases the need will have been defined clearly by the client and there will be little room for manoeuvre. If that is so you may consider merging the *Understanding of the need* with the *Terms of reference*. On other occasions the needs analysis may have to be very detailed, especially if it involves educating the client about subjects with which they are unfamiliar.

While every *Understanding of the need* is different, here is a general format which can be applied to most types of project.

Begin with a mini-summary if the section is very long (e.g. more than 5 pages)

The mini-summary should encapsulate what was already known about the need or current situation when you started, how you approached the needs analysis, what you now perceive the need to be, and how it should be met. If you are concerned about revealing all your recommendations too early remember that you are not writing a detective story. Many of your readers will be impatient to know the answers.

Thus an *Understanding of the need* section containing the detailed results of a questionnaire survey might begin like this:

> Sunningdale Systems have already identified the need for better communication of the company's short- and long-term objectives to staff at all levels of the company. They have specifically asked for proposals for a staff newsletter and for any other activities which would help to raise staff awareness of, and motivation to achieve, company objectives.
>
> Corporate Communications Ltd have analysed this need further through discussions with managers at all levels and a questionnaire survey of office and shop-floor staff. As a result, we have generated a list of recommendations for internal communications activities which we believe will communicate the company's objectives to the staff effectively and economically. A clear understanding of the company's objectives will improve morale and increase productivity.
>
> Corporate Communications recommend that Sunningdale Systems produce not only a monthly newsletter, but also a personalized mission statement for each member of staff, a revised company handbook, and a regular video programme.

Bring all readers up to the same educational level

Before you begin the detail of the needs analysis consider whether all your readers will understand what you are going to discuss, or whether the terms you are going to use will be familiar to them. You might want to have a section called *'Background'*, or perhaps something more informative (see below). The last thing you want is to lose the contract because someone in authority didn't know precisely what was meant by 'total quality management,' or 'virtual reality'. You need not be afraid of boring your more knowledgeable readers if you keep the educational background as a discrete section – after all, if they know it, they can easily skip over it.

Thus, you might include subheadings like:

What is BS5750?

Total quality management – a definition

CD-ROM – the training tool for the 1990s

If necessary, say how you approached the needs analysis
If you used any special techniques to analyse the need now is the time to say so. If you just thought about and discussed it there is no need to comment.

State what you understand the need to be
This seems obvious but it is surprising how often the statement of the need is lost in the supporting arguments. Be bold. Be clear. Be concise. State the need with conviction. Often, a bullet-pointed list will help.

Compconsult believe that Skisave Holidays urgently needs modifications to its information systems to:

- eliminate repetition of data input
- allow immediate data transfer between the booking and billing departments.

Recommendations

The next step is to tell the client how you plan to meet their need. This can often be merged with the *Project plan* (see below). Alternatively it can stand alone or form part of the *Understanding the need* section. Here's how to underline the logic and the worth of your recommendations.

State each recommendation confidently, clearly, and concisely
At this stage, there is no need to go into detail of exactly how each step in meeting the need will work – save this for your *Project plan* section. Your objective at this point is to help the client understand that your proposal is a rational, practical, effective response to their needs.

Compconsult recommend that Skisave Holidays' needs are met by:

- Installation of new PCs in the booking department
- Establishment of a Local Area Network between all departments
- Development of new order-processing software
- Training of all staff to use the new system.

Make your recommendations strong and specific – avoid sounding half-hearted about what you are trying to sell. Try to link each recommendation to a client benefit and, where possible, differentiate it from what you think your competitors may be offering. Thus:

> To achieve maximum sales for your product, we recommend a series of three mailings one month apart.

is likely to sound more convincing than ...

> One possible strategy that might work is a series of three or four mailings, perhaps one month apart.

Support your recommendations with facts, arguments and expert opinions

It is worth taking time and space to explain to the client why your recommendations meet their needs, especially if:

- you have been working to a very vague or open brief
- your definition of the need differs significantly from what the client thinks they need
- you are proposing to do more than the client thinks they need.

Let's examine how you can use facts, arguments and expert opinions to back up your definition of the need.

Why use a three-stage mailing programme?
[Fact] Research has shown that direct mail campaigns for this type of product can expect a 2–3% response for the first mailing, a further 2–3% for a second mailing, and a further 1–2% for a third mailing.

[Argument] On the basis of these statistics the additional *profit* generated by a second and third mailing could total more than £100,000. Merrivale Marketing therefore believe that the £10,000 cost of each additional mailing would be well justified.

[Expert opinion] Our opinion on the effectiveness of repeat mailings is shared by the Institute of Direct Marketing, whose director Camilla Mossworthy was recently quoted in the *Financial Times* as saying 'Direct marketing works best when it is carefully orchestrated. People may wonder why they keep receiving the same brochure for the same product, but the fact is, that's what brings in the sales.'

Note the heading 'Why use a three-stage mailing campaign?' When supporting your statement of the need think about the questions that will be in the client's mind and answer them convincingly. Don't be afraid to tackle potential areas of disagreement or to imagine which areas your client might be cynical about.

Project plan

Having established the need, and made your recommendations, you can then move on to say exactly how you will carry out those recommendations. You can think of the recommendations as strategy and the *Project plan* as tactics. This section is the 'nitty gritty' of the project – it tells the client exactly what they will be getting for their money. It may also form the basis for a contract, once agreed by both client and supplier.

When to be comprehensive ...
The content and length of the *Project plan* will obviously vary widely between projects. If you are planning a conference, for example, the project plan will be full of details of venues, mailings, speakers, accommodation and catering. It will have to be comprehensive so that the client will know what they are getting for their money and will be able to make fair comparisons between your proposal and that of your competitors.

And when not to ...

On the other hand if you are a management consultant trying to win the right to spend time in the client's company analysing their problems and writing a report, you should keep the *Project plan* fairly brief for two reasons. You do not want to make premature judgements, nor do you want to give away free consulting. In such a case the *Project plan* will be quite short – just a summary of your proposed approach: who you will talk to, how long it will take, what help you will expect from the client, and what goals you will achieve.

To ensure that the *Project plan* is complete, it's a good idea to use Kipling's 'six honest serving men'. Your *Project plan* should aim to answer the following questions:

- *What* are you going to do?
- *How* are you going to do it?
- *Why* are you doing it (in other words, what will it achieve for the client)?
- *Who* will execute each part of the project?
- *Where* will each part of the project take place?
- *When* will each step of the project happen?

Here's a simple example from a proposal for a company newsletter:

> [WHAT] Each monthly issue of the company newsletter will contain a two-page feature entitled *On site*, which will describe interesting and topical features of different Blockbuster Engineering sites around the UK. [WHY] This will help to generate reader interest in sites other than their own and to pave the way for the proposed inter-site 'jobswop' programme next year.
>
> [HOW] *On site* will be generated through interviews, with the emphasis on interesting personalities – shopfloor as well as management. [WHO] The interviews and accompanying photographs will normally be conducted by a Corporate Communications journalist, who will liaise with the personnel department at each site to find suitable interviewees. [WHERE and WHEN] The journalist will make a two-day visit to each site to obtain the interview. The sites proposed for the first three issues are ...

And another one from a management consultancy:

> [WHY] To evaluate the training needs of middle managers [HOW] a series of training needs workshops will be held [WHEN] during January and February 1995. [WHAT] These workshops will take the form of half-day sessions combining individual evaluations and structured group discussions, [WHO] facilitated by Nigel Coxton, our training specialist. [WHERE] We suggest that these sessions are held off-site in a nearby hotel, to avoid disruption by everyday problems and activities.

Note that in the *Project plan* section of the proposal the questions 'who' and 'when' can be answered quite briefly, if you have separate sections elsewhere for *Personnel* and *Schedules*. It is not advisable to leave the question of who and when out of the *Project plan* altogether, however – it breaks the flow of your sales pitch if readers are continually flicking back and forth in the proposal to find the answers to their questions. If you have separate sections elsewhere in the proposal for *Credentials* or *Schedules*, make sure you cross-refer to them in the *Project plan*. *You* may think it's obvious that they are there, but your readers may need a reminder.

Be specific, sales-oriented and succinct

Be specific   The more precise you can be in the *Project plan* about what the client will receive for their money, the more confident they will be that you know what you are doing and can deliver the goods.

Another important reason for being very specific is so that you can be compared fairly with your competitors. Many a good proposal has lost out because clients did not realize that they were not comparing like with like.

Be sales-oriented   Remember that you are writing the proposal to sell the project, not to list all that you can do. The golden rule is: think about what each component does for the client, not just about what it is. In other words emphasize the benefits, rather than just describing the features (more about this in Chapter 7).

Another way of making sure your *Project plan* is sales-oriented is to think about the competition and what they might be offering. Place special emphasis on services which you believe are unique to you, or where you have a distinct advantage.

Be succinct Though the proposal plan should be detailed, think about which details are really important for the client to make an informed buying decision. On the one hand, you want to provide answers to all the usual questions, almost before the client has thought of them. On the other hand, you do not want them to drown in distracting detail. Consider whether some types of information, especially the very technical, would be better placed in the *Appendices* at the back of the proposal.

Schedules

Completion of the project on time is usually one of the client's first considerations – at least as important, if not more, than keeping within the budget. Clients are often quite tense about the whole subject of scheduling, for a variety of possible reasons:

- The success of the client's business may depend on this particular project being completed on time. Other projects may not be able to start until it is completed. If you let your client down, they may well end up letting their own customers down.
- The personal prestige and image of the person who commissioned the proposal may be dependent on this project being completed on time. Individuals may have made bold promises to their colleagues. They need your help to ensure those promises are not broken.
- The client may be well aware that they have left it rather late in the day to brief an external supplier; perhaps they thought they could do the job themselves but then ran out of time.

The *Schedules* section is therefore not just a matter of telling the client how long it is likely to take to complete each stage of the project. It is also a selling tool.

Be realistic, reassuring and readable

Be realistic Don't underestimate the time needed in the hope that it will help you to win the job. This will usually backfire on you. An astute client will recognize your estimates as unrealistic and cross you off the shortlist without a second thought. Or, if you win the job, you will then be wrong-footed from day one and risk antagonizing the client permanently. If the proposal is later used as the basis of a contract, you will be faced with the prospect of making embarrassing revisions to the schedule, or signing a contract you know you can't fulfil.

Be reassuring Although the schedule should be realistic, there is no reason why it should be pessimistic. The main presentation of the schedule should usually be based on the 'best-case scenario', assuming no hold-ups or unforeseen circumstances.

Most schedules are best presented in terms of working days rather than specific dates, thus avoiding the need to make endless revisions until the start date of the project is firmly established.

Make sure that you add suitable provisos wherever the schedule is dependent on the client providing something, or some other factor that is truly beyond your control. For example:

> Note: this schedule assumes two weeks for client approval of the draft manuscript of the annual report, and one week for approval of page proofs.

You can tie your working-days schedule into a few specific dates to give the client a rough idea of what will happen in practice, with statements like:

> Assuming a start date of 11 January 1996, the counter displays will be ready for delivery on 14 May, two weeks before the start of the summer sales campaign.

Be readable Make sure that your schedule is understandable at a glance. This is only courteous to the client and helps to promote the professional image of your company. There are several ways in which you can ensure that your schedule is easy to read and understand.

- *Use charts and tables, especially for complex projects* Many project management software programs produce such charts (Gantt charts) automatically. To help the client even further, you could highlight key steps in colour or bold type. Or you could use colour to distinguish between different parts of the project or different participants. This is particularly useful if you wish to draw the client's attention to critical points where they will have to make a decision or take action.
- *Be selective – show only what is relevant to the client* There may be many stages in the project which the client neither needs nor wants to know about. These internal activities may be very important to the success of the project and of great interest to people within *your* organization. Unless they are also meaningful to the client, however, restrict them to your own internal documentation. As with charts and tables, you can highlight key steps with bold type or underlining.
- *Consider providing a 'dates for your diary' section* If the schedule is necessarily long and complex, the client will appreciate a summary of key dates. This makes the client feel good because it demonstrates that you have thought about their needs and concerns. If the client is setting a tight deadline, the 'dates for your diary' section is also useful as a polite way of alerting the client to their own responsibilities, for example:

  – to give a prompt go-ahead to their chosen supplier
  – to supply information, attend meetings, or make decisions at key points during the life of the project.

Costs

The bare minimum that should be contained in the *Costs* section should be:

- a statement of the total cost of the job
- a brief statement of what is included (i.e. what they will receive for their money)

- a brief statement of what is excluded (e.g. VAT, expenses)
- a note about proposed payment terms (e.g. if you are expecting stage payments).

Thus a simple statement of costs might read:

Total cost for a two-day time management course for up to 12 delegates:	£XXXX plus VAT.
Included:	<ul><li>services of two tutors</li><li>bound course notes for each delegate</li><li>tutors' travelling and accommodation expenses</li></ul>
Not included:	venue hire and catering (to be recharged to client at cost)
Payment terms:	30 days from delivery

Cost breakdown

In many proposals, however, you will be expected to provide a further breakdown of costs. This *can* act in your favour. A cost breakdown will:

- demonstrate exactly what the client is paying for at each stage of the project, so that you can be compared with the competition on equal terms. Otherwise, another firm could put forward a similar or lower estimate and the client would have no way of knowing they would not be getting the same product or level of service as you would provide.
- offer an opportunity for you to demonstrate accuracy and scrupulous attention to detail regarding costs, which will help to convince the client that you are a supplier to be trusted.
- show what each phase or part of the project will cost – useful for the client who may be reluctant to buy the whole thing, but may agree to commission a smaller part of your overall proposal.

However, the cost breakdown also has its pitfalls. It:

- often takes a great deal of time and effort to prepare.
- can be hard for the client to understand – leading to a general feeling of confusion and irritation and the potential for misunderstandings.
- allows the client to quibble over small details either now or at a later phase of the project.
- allows the client to calculate exactly where you make most of your profit – which you may well feel is none of their business.
- could conceivably fall into the hands of your competitors via a naive or unscrupulous client, allowing them to compete with you on unfair terms.

You can guard against some of the pitfalls of cost breakdowns by using the following techniques:

Keep as much as possible on file   Previous proposals can often be 'recycled', saving you the trouble of costing everything from first principles. Similarly, many consulting companies can work out standard tables of, say, costs per day for consultants at different grades.

Lay it out carefully   Careful tabulation of costs will help the client to see what they are receiving for their money. (For more details on laying out tables, see Chapter 11.)

Be specific about hours and rates for different grades of personnel   If much of the cost of the project is in the time of the individuals involved, give a detailed breakdown of how many hours/days senior and junior staff are expected to work and their hourly/daily rates. This usually creates a more credible impression than averaging out the rates of different grades of staff. Clients have a right to know exactly what they're paying for.

Use a costs summary   A brief summary of the *main* costs of the project will be extremely helpful to clients who don't want to be bogged down in detail. It can also be circulated alongside the overall summary to people who will not be willing to read the whole proposal, but may nevertheless have an important impact on the decision to buy.

Be aware of client psychology   Think about which costs the client is likely to find hardest to swallow. In researching this book I found that many clients were most likely to quibble with the 'consultant's expenses' section of the costs, not because this was the most important, but because it was an area where clients felt most irritated by what they saw as rip-offs. You may be able to identify other areas in your speciality which are likely to be subjected to especially careful scrutiny.

If you think the client will quibble with a particular set of costs, be sure to provide sufficient explanation to enable them to see exactly what they are paying for. If you are a firm of management consultants, for example, it will normally be to your advantage to break down the total costs of your time to show how much attention the client is getting from the most senior members of your team, how much time you expect to spend inside the client's company, and so on.

Follow the client's instructions to the letter   When proposing for large contracts, particularly in the public sector, you may be asked to break down costs in a particular way – for example, man-months or man-days. Follow these instructions to the letter. If you don't, the client can, and often will, reject the whole proposal simply on the basis of non-compliance.

As described below, some large public-sector organizations now ask for costs to be provided in a totally separate document – the *Financial proposal*. As this is the foundation of their selection system, it is in your interests to do exactly what they ask.

Other aspects you may need to cover in your *Costs* section include:

- *'Estimates' statement*   If you are a management consultant, for example, you may expect the client to treat your costs as an estimate rather than a firm price, because there is no way of knowing at the outset exactly how much work is involved. If so, make sure you state this, but make it clear that you understand you have a responsibility to keep costs down.

- *'Variables' statement*   Usually, it is better to allow a little leeway in your costs so that you can absorb a few extra hours or a slight increase in the prices charged by your suppliers without referring back to the client. Clients tend to feel they are getting good value for money if you are able to do the job for a fixed price with no quibbles. In some circumstances, however, you may wish to make a statement that certain prices quoted may vary according to specified circumstances. For example, you may be unable to predict the prices charged by outside suppliers far enough in advance. Or you may have worked with the client before and know that they have a tendency to redesign the project as they go along.

This price assumes one set of client amendments to page proofs and one to colour proofs. Additional time spent on amendments will be charged at £40 per hour.

This price assumes a sufficient number of delegates to occupy the whole of the hotel. If the number of delegates is less than 200, the room rate may increase. These charges will be passed on to the client at cost plus 5%.

Your proposed project plan might involve someone from the client's company on a full-time or part-time basis for a specified period. If so, estimate their time and make sure you state that it is not included in your cost estimate.

Should you allow room in your prices for negotiation?
Only your own experience will tell you whether your client will accept the costs as quoted, or whether they are likely to quibble over every detail or try to beat you down on price. If you predict these problems you might adjust your prices to allow a little room for manoeuvre. On the other hand it may be more professional to offer your best price and stick to it. If the client then insists on a price reduction, say that it can only be achieved

if certain parts of the project are omitted or if the client undertakes to perform more of the work themselves.

Two-way price negotiation is much more likely in the private sector. For any project where quality counts, the decision is unlikely to be made on the basis of price alone. Tough clients are quite likely to select the proposal that appeals most and try to beat that supplier down towards the price of the lowest quote.

The public sector also takes account of quality in varying ways, but there tends to be less room for negotiation. It is more a matter of pitching the price right in the first place. If taking part in competitive tendering in the public sector, you must find out how the selection is made (public bodies are obliged to tell you).

One notorious approach, thankfully rare when selecting professional services, is the double-envelope system. In this system a technical and a financial proposal are submitted in separate envelopes. The technical proposals are opened first and the first round selects proposals that meet a minimum quality standard. The second round decides between them purely on the basis of price.

Fortunately, selection of suppliers of professional services is likely to be made on a modified version of this system. Those proposals that reach the minimum quality standard are assigned scores for technical merit before they go forward to the second round. When the financial proposals are opened the technical scores are then weighted by a financial score and the one with the best overall score wins. This can be a very fair system, ensuring that a proposal cannot win on price alone, and that the selection committee cannot be biased by knowing prices beforehand.The more you know about how much weight the different scores carry in this kind of system, the more accurately you will be able to pitch your price.

Personnel and Credentials

These sections can play such an important part in selling your services that specific techniques for writing them are covered in Chapter 8. Here is just a brief summary.

- Proposal CVs are not like job applications. Keep them to less than a page (half a page is often enough), and stick to *relevant* experience and qualifications.
- Use your SWOT and key competitive advantage analyses to provide a framework for the *Credentials*. Stress the benefits to the client, not just how great you think your company is.
- Don't expect your credentials to be the same for each client. They will vary according to the client's needs and priorities.
- Use examples, mini-case histories and names of past clients to underline your credibility.
- Substantiate promotional statements with hard facts.

The way forward

There is no need for a *Conclusion* in a proposal. The *Summary* will have outlined all the important points you need to make. However, you might like to finish off with a few lines saying what you expect to happen next. For example:

Belforth Associates believe that the public relations strategy we have proposed will help to establish Ashingden Health Services as the leading healthcare provider in the north-east. If you have any queries about any aspect of this proposal, please call Linda Belforth on 051 738 9980. We look forward to hearing your response to these ideas and would welcome the opportunity to present them in more detail at a meeting at your offices at a mutually convenient time.

Appendices

The *Appendices* section is the place to put any information which will not be of interest to the key decision makers, but might be of interest to a few readers or serve as useful back-up when queries arise. Materials that might be included as *Appendices* include:

- detailed technical specifications
- examples of paperwork such as timesheets
- complex scheduling charts (give a simplified version in the main proposal)

- very detailed cost breakdowns that will only be of interest to one or two of your readers
- detailed case histories.

How long should a proposal be?

Keep it short ...

A proposal should be just as long as is necessary to sell the project, and no more. In researching this book, I found that one of the commonest complaints clients made about proposals was that they were 'too long and full of waffle'. In fact I have never heard anyone complain that a proposal was too short, though I have heard them say 'it didn't have enough meat on it', meaning it didn't have enough detail to support its arguments.

Some consulting companies think that if a proposal is long and weighty it will seem serious and will therefore be taken seriously. This is not the case. Most clients can recognize 'padding' pretty quickly and become very irritated with it. The most precious commodity for most business people is time. Readers want to extract the information from a document as quickly as possible. They don't want to wade through great lakes of stagnant prose looking for little islands of relevant information.

Think of your readers and keep your proposal as short as is compatible with providing all the information necessary to support your argument. There are three reasons why proposal length gets out of control. The proposal may be:

- *Too wordy – full of empty statements*   This can be cured by a disciplined approach to writing and some tough editing once the proposal is complete.
- *Full of unnecessary repetition*   Some repetition of key points is constructive and helpful to your reader. But inadvertent repetition, due to poor organization or sloppy writing, is a surefire way of irritating your readers. Better planning in advance, and ruthless editing later, will cure this problem.
- *Full of unnecessary facts, thoughts and arguments*   The key test for every piece of information in your proposal is: does this

help me to sell? If it does, put it in – somewhere. If it helps to sell, but only to a small proportion of the readers, then consider putting the information into an *Appendix*.

... but include enough detail to support your arguments

Some projects, especially those of a highly technical nature, will require long proposals. There is nothing intrinsically wrong with a long proposal if every word is meaningful, but you will have to take special care to make it easy for the client to find their way around the proposal. You can do this by structuring it in a reader-friendly way, providing interim summaries of key points and using plenty of helpful 'signposts' such as headings and cross-references to help them find the information they need in the shortest time possible. (See Chapter 4 for more information on structuring and signposting.)

Mini-proposals and sales letters

Mini-proposals and sales letters can be structured in exactly the same way as the comprehensive proposal, leaving out and merging sections as necessary. Thus, for a mini-proposal, you might have:

- covering letter
- Title page / *Table of contents*
- *Introduction / Terms of reference / Understanding of the need*
- *Recommendations / Project plan*
- *Schedules*
- *Costs*
- *Personnel*
- *Credentials* 'Why use Smith and Brown Associates?'
- *The way forward.*

You could put the same information into a sales letter, which is basically a covering letter and mini-proposal rolled into one. There would be no title page, but the letter would contain subheadings based on the main proposal sections. The sales letter can start and end with the same elements as the covering letter (see Chapter 13). Thus it would contain:

- a friendly opening
- a statement of what is included in the letter
- the proposal itself (with subheadings)
- what happens next
- a friendly close.

Summary

Most proposals will contain sections corresponding to those below, though you may want to merge sections, and/or give them more interesting headings.

- *Summary* – must give the client a clear idea of what they're buying, and why they should buy it from you (see Chapter 9 for more detail).

- *Introduction* – who you are, what you're proposing, and for whom.

- *Terms of reference* – can often be merged with the introduction.

- *Understanding of the need* – content varies with the client.

- *Recommendations* – confident, clear and concise.

- *Project plan* – who, what, how, where, why and when; specific, sales-oriented and succinct.

- *Schedules* – realistic, reassuring and readable.

- *Costs* – follow the client's instructions to the letter

- *Personnel* and *Credentials* – see Chapter 8 for full details.

- *The way forward* – suggest the next step.

Action points

1   Review the structure of a recent or current proposal:

   – Have you included a *Summary*?
   – Are needs and recommendations clearly defined?
   – Can the client see at a glance exactly what they are getting for their money?
   – Is there any matter included in the main body of the proposal that would be better placed in *Appendices*?

2   Consider your five most recent proposals and evaluate their length. Are they too long and unwieldy? Could you make them easier for the client to read by:

   – editing out some material altogether?
   – moving some material to *Appendices*?
   – using interim summaries?
   – using more informative headings and subheadings?

3   Ask yourself:

   – What is our overall success rate? Is our investment of time in writing proposals repaid by the amount of business we win?
   – Do we have the right balance between the number of comprehensive proposals we prepare, and the number of mini-proposals or sales letters?
   – Are we going into too much/not enough detail?
   – Could we increase our success rate by doing more short, speculative, proposals or sales letters?
   – Could we increase our efficiency by doing shorter proposals?

4 Thinking and writing logically

You've researched your proposal, decided on your marketing strategy for the project and decided what sections your proposal should contain. Now you're ready to write. Let's begin to think about *how* your proposal should be written.

In my view, a proposal should be:

- well-organized (this chapter)
- client-friendly (Chapter 5)
- clear (Chapter 6)
- persuasive and powerful (Chapter 7).

Good organization is fundamental to effective proposal writing, or any other kind of writing for that matter. When people complain that something is 'badly written', what they often mean is that it is badly organized. Without good organization you cannot achieve the other key qualities of client-friendliness, clarity and power.

Well-organized writing allows the reader to follow the flow of your ideas so easily that agreeing with your suggestions comes naturally. In contrast, badly organized writing leaves your reader in doubt about what you're trying to sell and why, and so they will be disinclined to buy. In addition, if your writing is badly organised, your reader might suspect that the service you supply will also be badly organized.

Let's consider some ideas for thinking and writing logically that will increase the power of your proposals.

The need for logic and order in writing

We all make sense of the world we see, touch and hear by sorting and classifying objects and ideas into manageable-sized groups and arranging them in some kind of logical order. The more sophisticated we are in our thinking, the more we try to classify things. Thus a baby might register *animals*. A toddler will have sorted them into *cats*, *dogs*, *rabbits* and so on. An adult will make finer distinctions like *labrador*, *rottweiler* and *chihuahua*.

People will always try to impose some structure on the world around them. Let us not delve into the psychology of why some people are only happy if all the yellow pencils are lined up on the righthand side of the desk. Suffice it to say that, within reason, most people are happiest when things are neatly sorted and classified.

Reading is no exception. Readers expect to see some kind of logic in a string of words and sentences. If none is apparent the human mind will naturally seek to impose a structure.

When writing a proposal you should aim to do all the sorting and classifying for your readers. There are two key reasons for this. A well-organized proposal:

- helps your readers by reducing the strain on their brains
- enables you to get across the message you want rather than leaving them to draw their own conclusions.

Not many people think in a highly organized way, progressing neatly from the beginning to the end of a problem or idea. On the contrary, most of us jump around mentally from one subject to another, throwing up new ideas and trains of thought as we go. This is as it should be. Creativity would be stifled if we tried to regiment our thoughts into single file. It is when we begin to write that we start to impose structure and order.

You will need to think about structure both before and during the writing of your proposal. Structure can be imposed at several different levels:

- the sections you choose to include in your proposal
- within main sections or chapters
- within subsections dealing with different ideas or arguments
- within paragraphs
- within sentences.

Deciding on your main sections or chapters is fairly easy and we have already discussed this in Chapter 3. When you are structuring the remainder of the proposal, unless you are following a very specific official format, you will have a free hand. So how do you cope when you sit down at a blank sheet of paper or computer screen?

Do you really need to organize at a detailed level before you start to write?

You may say 'I'm short of time, do I really have to do any more planning? Can't I get on with it and start writing? I'll just put it all down and sort it out later.' The answer – based on personal experience – is that careful organization nearly always saves you time in the long run.

The proposal writer who can sit down and write each section straight through is a very rare bird. The rest of us work more efficiently if we have worked out some kind of framework before we start writing. A framework within each main section helps you to:

- sell more effectively, because you can build logical arguments which are easy for your readers to follow
- write more quickly, because you already know what points you wish to include
- avoid missing out key points in the hurry of putting everything down on paper
- avoid writer's block, because you know what you are going to say.

Methods for clarifying and organizing your thoughts

Here are some methods you can use to help you clarify your thoughts and organize them into logical groups before you start to write. None is magic – just choose the one that works best for you. There is no 'right' way of devising a logical structure. What matters is that one eventually appears.

Mind mapping®

Mind mapping® is a technique developed by psychologist Tony Buzan and popularized in his many books. It is based on the concept of 'radiant thinking', which, Buzan argues, is the natural way of thinking. In real life, people do not think in hierarchically ordered structures. Instead, thought is unpredictable, moving around from topic to topic, building on previous ideas, and studded with occasional flashes of insight. Mind mapping provides a way of visualizing this process, so that you build a picture of your thoughts before you start to write, without being forced prematurely into any particular way of structuring your document.

Figure 4.1 shows a typical mind map for the *Credentials* section of a proposal. Once you have reached this stage, imposing a logical structure on each section becomes quite easy.

Mind mapping can be done by one person alone, but it is also an extremely effective technique for groups. Using a large whiteboard or flipchart the team can work together to develop an agreed structure for the whole of the proposal.

Books on mind mapping are listed in Further reading (see p. 241).

Pack of cards

Another structuring technique which allows you to think in a fairly random way at first is to jot down your key topics in note form on small white file cards or Post-it notes. You can then lay out the cards or notes and use them to build your structure.

Listing headings

Many of you will be familiar with the idea of listing all the main headings and subheadings you might like to use and shuffling

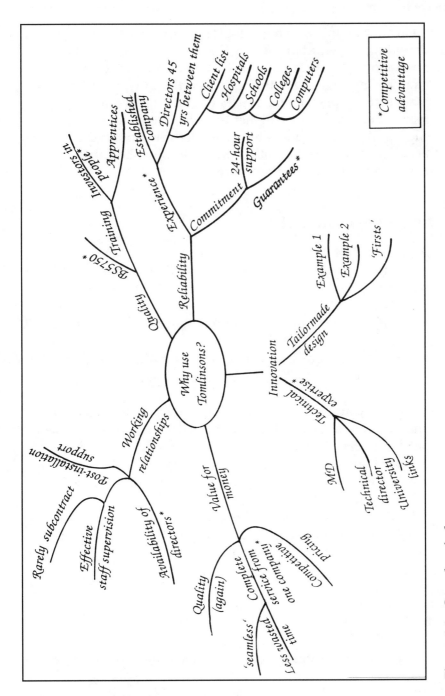

Figure 4.1 Sample mind map

them around until you find a logical structure. This is easy if you are sitting at a word processor. The only warning I would like to give about this technique is that it does tend to encourage straight-line thinking – the temptation is to work through the main sections one at a time without stopping to think how they relate to each other or whether they need to be there at all. So, I suggest that you use this technique to 'tidy up' after you have been through one of the other processes described above which allow your thoughts to flow more freely.

Setting a page budget

A page budget is simply a plan estimating a certain number of pages for the proposal and for each section within it. Setting a page budget is essential for two reasons. It will help you to:

- avoid wasting time and resources writing more text than you need
- assign the right amount of text to each section, in other words, to obtain a balance of topics.

How do you set a page budget? Many large public-sector organizations set a limit for you. If not, it is up to you to work one out for yourself. Usually you will have some idea of what is expected and acceptable. If in doubt remember that one of the commonest complaints from clients is that proposals are longer than they need to be.

Having estimated the total number of pages you can allocate rough numbers of pages to each section. Usually you will need one page for each of the following:

- title page
- *Summary*
- *Table of contents.*

The rest of the pages should be allocated bearing in mind the following questions:

- *What sections do you need?* Chapter 3 discusses the standard proposal plan, but you may decide you do not need all of these sections.
- *Which sections will be most important/interesting to your client?* It's tempting to concentrate on those sections that are interesting to you, or where it's relatively easy to provide a lot of detail. But think about whether your client might be more interested in other topics. You want to demonstrate your ability to understand their problems and offer creative cost-effective solutions. You're also aiming to answer their questions, almost before they ask them.
- *How much detail should you provide in each section?* This will vary with the project. Some may require the needs analysis/understanding in detail. With others it may be enough simply to refer back to the detailed brief you have already been given. Likewise the *Project plan* for a management consultancy project is often quite brief – after all, you do not want to give all your methodology away beforehand. In contrast, the *Project plan* for a civil engineering project will contain many pages of technical detail.
- *Are there any large diagrams or charts?* Don't forget to allow space for these in your page budget.

There are no hard and fast rules about how many pages each section should take. The important thing is that the balance between the sections should be right and should reflect the client's interests.

If you are tempted to just start writing and see how your proposal grows, consider the experience of Macdonnell Douglas, the US aerospace giant. They found that a page budget system saved them millions of dollars by cutting the time it took to prepare technical reports. Page budgeting can save time and money on proposals too.

Organizing at the detailed level

Despite meticulous planning you won't have your thoughts 100 per cent organized before committing them to paper or word processor. There is nothing wrong with this. For most of us it is easier to fine-tune the organization of our thoughts once they have been made visible.

Too often, however, proposal writers do not spend enough time sorting their thoughts into a logical order that takes the reader by the hand and leads them through the argument from beginning to end. Remember – to be helpful to your reader you must do all the sorting and classifying for them. The reader should have to do as little mental work as possible.

You can do the fine-tuning of your organization at two stages: as you write, or after you have completed the whole of the first draft. Some people find it bolsters their confidence to have the whole proposal, or at least all the main sections, on paper before they start to fine-tune the organization. Others prefer to go back and tinker with each section almost as soon as it is written. Neither method is wrong – just choose the one that works best for you. As you develop into a more practised proposal writer you will probably find that your first drafts are becoming better organized, because you can see the structure more clearly in your mind. (See Chapter 12 for more thoughts on the revision process and how to make it more efficient.)

Let's consider a practical example of organization at the detailed level. How often have you read something like this?

Corporate communications at Smith's Widgets are currently managed by the Publicity Department who are responsible for both internal and external communications, and produce an employee magazine, the annual report and the company brochure. The department is headed by the Director of Publicity and employs three staff. They are also responsible for producing customer mailings, for commissioning advertising through ad agencies and for producing PR material through their PR agency. In addition, they also produce product brochures for the WondaWidget range of products, regular newsletters for the workforce of the Dunbridge and Wellington plants and are responsible for the quarterly 'News from Smith's Widgets', which is sent to customers.

The writer has just put down thoughts in the order that they first came to mind. Reasonable for a first draft perhaps, but it needs a more logical structure to make it reader-friendly. A little extra work will give you something like this:

> Corporate communications at Smith's Widgets are managed by the Publicity Department, which is headed by the Director of Publicity and employs three staff. They are responsible for internal communications, including an employee magazine and regular newsletters for the Dunbridge and Wellington plants. They are also responsible for external communications, including the annual report, the company brochure, product brochures for the Wonda-Widget range, customer mailings and the quarterly customer newsletter 'News from Smith's Widgets'. In addition, they commission advertising and public relations from specialist agencies.

or even better ...

> Corporate communications at Smith's Widgets are managed by the Publicity Department, which is headed by the Director of Publicity and employs three staff. They are responsible for:
>
> **Internal communications**
> - quarterly employee magazine
> - monthly newsletters for the Dunbridge and Wellington plants
>
> **External communications**
> - annual report
> - product brochures for the WondaWidget range
> - customer mailings
> - quarterly customer newsletter 'News from Smith's Widgets'
> - advertising and public relations (commissioned from specialist agencies)

Note how, in this third version, headings and lists have been used to underline the logic of the structure. This makes it easy for readers to understand the key messages quickly and painlessly.

Different types of logical order

Your proposal will have most impact if you think carefully about the flow of your argument and how you can express it by arranging your subsections in a logical order. Remember that if you don't do this, readers may make unwarranted assumptions about why you have put a certain section in a certain place. The appropriate logical order will depend on the section you are writing and the effect you are trying to create.

Some common choices are:

- in order of importance – always a powerful arrangement
- in chronological order – usual in the project plan section
- in categorical order – for example, the Smith's Widgets example above grouped communications into Internal and External.

More examples of logical ordering are given in the section on *'Lists'* below.

Underlining your logic with headings and subheadings

Headings and subheadings are essential in almost any kind of business writing. They enhance the readability, clarity and impact of any document – not just proposals and reports, but also memos and even letters.

Headings serve four purposes. They:

- act as signposts, enabling readers to find their way around the proposal quickly and easily
- attract attention to key points
- provide visual relief
- may be used to skim-read the proposal.

The main chapter headings of your proposal may be dictated to you, for example by government regulations. Private sector clients may also have certain expectations of the main chapter headings, (see Chapter 3). However, you will have a free hand in devising subheadings.

How can you make the most of headings? Here are some tips.

Use headings to sell

In all but the most formal proposals, make the most of your opportunity to use 'selling' headings and subheadings.

Thus these formal headings:

(Section heading) **Credentials**

(Subheadings) **Company history**

Recent projects

Might become:

(Section heading) **Why use Geoscan?**

(Subheadings) **Three decades of experience in the oil industry**

Up-to-date expertise

Make headings specific and illuminating

There is no reason why headings should consist of only one or two words when more information would be useful. For example, it might be more helpful and informative to write 'Advantages of customized project management software' rather than just 'Advantages'.

In this example if you were going into considerable detail about the various advantages you might have subheadings for each one. Assuming that the tone of your proposal was fairly informal, you might consider even more informative subheads. These could be one-sentence statements such as 'Greater flexibility' or 'Easier to operate'.

Avoid excessively long headings

Headings should usually occupy only one line and certainly never more than two. Very long headings are unattractive and difficult to read. Remember that even informative headings do not have to be complete sentences.

Do not substitute headings for body text

Although some people will skim-read the document by reading the headings, others may not read them at all. If someone is very interested in a particular section they will be concentrating on the body text and may not take in the information in the headings. It is a bad idea to use the heading as if it were your introductory sentence.

Avoid:

Completion by 1 March
This will give us an opportunity to test the system thoroughly before the beginning of the new financial year.

Use something like this instead:

Completion by 1 March
The project will be completed by 1 March. This will give us an opportunity to test the system thoroughly before the beginning of the new financial year.

Indicate the hierarchy of your headings

Help your readers by making the most important headings the biggest. You can also change the font of the heading, though too many different fonts will make your proposal look 'bitty' and confused. (See Chapter 11 for more information on how to create a simple and effective hierarchy of headings using simple techniques available to anyone with a word-processor.)

Don't use too many levels of heading

The simplest arrangement is to have main headings and subheadings (first and second order headings), for example:

First order heading: **Proposed project plan**

Second order headings: **System design**

However in all but the shortest proposals you might want to include third order headings, for example:

First order heading: **Proposed project plan**

Second order heading: **System design**

Third order heading: *Hardware requirements*

If you use more than three levels of heading, including your main chapter headings, you are likely to confuse the reader. (See Chapter 11 for more information on how to choose an appropriate typeface for each order of heading.)

Number headings when there is a good reason
There are two good reasons for numbering headings:

- *When regulations demand it*. Numbered headings are often a requirement when proposing for the public sector.
- *In long and complex proposals, where you will want to refer to sections or paragraphs by number*. If you don't plan to refer to the numbers, however, it's pointless to use them.

Numbering should be consistent with your logical structure and with your first, second and third order headings. Limit your numbering system to a maximum of three tiers to correspond with your three levels of headings:

3   Proposed project plan

3.1   System design

3.1.1   *Hardware requirements*

One of the problems with using numbered sections is that when you add or delete a section you have to renumber the whole document. Some word-processing programs have the ability to renumber sections every time you make a change.

Use headings for visual relief

Headings help to break up the text into manageable chunks so that the reader does not feel overwhelmed by the amount of text. There should be at least one heading or subheading on every page. If you feel that more headings are inappropriate, try breaking up the text with a list instead.

Underlining your logic with lists

Lists are another important way of underlining your logic. They are useful because they:

- use fewer words than text written in full sentences
- make your logic plain
- attract attention to key points
- break up solid text and provide visual relief.

There is usually no reason to number the items in a list. 'Bullet points' (as used in this book), dashes or asterisks are often all you need to draw attention to each point. However, it may be useful to number lists if you are going to refer back to specific points or if you want to indicate sequential steps, for example:

Our proposed programme covers these seven steps:

1 Review of the existing system
2 Recommendations for change
3 Design of new software
4 Installation of new hardware
5 System testing
6 Staff training
7 Ongoing support

Remember that lists can consist of sentences, or even paragraphs. With these kinds of lists, you can use the first word, or the first few words, as an additional level of heading, highlighted in bold or italic type:

Using an external supplier offers many advantages, including:

- *Reduced overheads*   You do not need to set aside office space, pay staff, or buy and maintain equipment.
- *Greater flexibility*   You can obtain a wider range of services from an external supplier than from an in-house unit.
- *Quicker access*   You will not have to wait in a queue with other departments in your organization.

or an alternative 'breezier' style:

Using an external supplier can:

- *Reduce your overheads* – no need to set aside office space, pay staff, or buy and maintain equipment.
- *Give you flexibility* – with a wider range of services from an external supplier than an in-house unit could provide.
- *Speed up your operation* – instant access to services with no waiting your turn.

Note how each item in the list is structured in a similar way. In the first version the advantages are expressed as adjective–noun pairs. In the second version they're given as verb–[your]–noun combinations. The point I'm making is not to do with grammar – it's that each item is structured in a similar way which, because of the reader's urge to look for order, produces a satisfying effect. It also adds to the list's impact. This is known as *parallel structure* and can also be used within sentences. (See Chapter 6 for more about parallel structures.)

Your list should always have a logical order. You may want to order it chronologically, as in the numbered list example above. Or you may want to order it in terms of importance. Usually it is wise to give the most important point first – some readers won't read through to the end of the list, so make your key points early. For example, in the list above, the proposal writer has decided that 'reduced overheads' is the most convincing reason for using an external supplier, 'greater flexibility' the next most convincing and 'quicker access' probably the least convincing.

Where there is no particular order of priority, it's still better to use some kind of logical order, for example:

Categorical, for a computer project:

- Hardware requirements
- Software requirements
- Personnel requirements

Geographical, by sales regions:

- South-west
- South-east
- Midlands
- North
- Scotland
- Wales
- Northern Ireland

Structural, for an exhibition stand:

- External design
- Internal design
  - reception area
  - product display
  - sales area
  - services

Alphabetical:

- Aberystwyth
- Canterbury
- Manchester
- Wolverhampton

You must decide what logical order suits your particular list – the important thing is to avoid lists in random order. Because of the natural tendency of readers to look for logic and order in all things, they are likely to impose their own mental structure on a randomly ordered list, giving it an order of importance or sequence which you may not have intended.

Long lists

It's sometimes tempting to use very long lists. But this can mean that the impact of the list is lost. By the time they get to the end the readers will have lost interest. They will certainly have forgotten the other items in the list! So, if you have a very long list, break it into several logical sections each with its own subheading. Thus in a proposal for a conference management company, you might find a list like this:

> We can offer you a complete conference package to cover all the administration and management of your meeting. Our services include:
>
> **Planning**
> - Conference planning and academic support
> - Advice on speakers and speaker liaison
> - Budget preparation and account management
>
> **Promotion**
> - Mailing and database compilation
> - Sponsorship sourcing
> - Publicity and advertising
> - Advance registration
>
> **Logistics**
> - Venue sourcing
> - Hotel or college accommodation
> - Catering support
> - Exhibitions and displays
> - Social programmes, excursions and tours
>
> **On-site management**
> - Pre-prints, programmes, binders and badges
> - Delegate registration and welcome
> - Technical and audio-visual support
> - Translation and interpretation
>
> **Follow-up**
> - Post-conference reports and proceedings

No more than seven items for maximum memorability

Is there a maximum number of items you should include in a list? Well, according to psychologists, most people can only hold a maximum of seven items in their short-term memory. So, if you want your readers to view the list as a whole, there are good psychological reasons for limiting it to no more than seven items. If you have a very long list, you can often break it up into several sublists under different headings, as described above.

Summary

- Think, then organize, then write.

- Try mind mapping or related techniques.

- Always set a page budget.

- Use plenty of headings and subheadings – at least one per page, often more.

- Size/typestyle of headings should indicate their place in the hierarchy of ideas.

- If possible, use headings to sell.

- Make headings specific and illuminating, but not too long.

- Number headings only if you are going to use the numbers (or if regulations demand it).

- Use lists to underline the logical structure and to break up solid blocks of text.

- Break up long lists into manageable chunks.

Action points

1   For your next proposal try mind mapping for the whole proposal, or for just one of the sections. If it helps to clarify your thoughts or saves time, keep doing it!

2   For your next proposal, set a page budget before you start to write. Did you find it helped you manage your time?

3   Study one of your current or recent proposals. Go through and highlight the headings.

   – Are there enough headings?
   – Have you used first, second and third order headings with the right emphasis?
   – Have you arranged subsections in a logical order?
   – Do headings help to sell?
   – Are headings specific and informative?
   – Are any of the headings too long? (They should usually be no more than one line.)

4   Look at your lists.

   – Have you used bullet points or numbers appropriately?
   – Have you subdivided long lists?
   – Are the items each in a logical order?
   – Are there any blocks of solid text that would be better as a list?

5 Client-friendly writing

An understanding of how people read business documents – in other words, a bit of reader psychology – is one of the factors that will give your proposal a competitive edge.

Understanding your readers and writing your proposal to suit is not cynical manipulation; it's an important aspect of customer service. If the proposal makes the client feel comfortable and makes their life easier, they'll be grateful. What is more, they'll receive the subliminal impression that you care about your clients and share their view of the world.

Writing your proposal so that it is as easy as possible to read and understand is not an insult. It does not imply that you think your client is incapable of understanding something difficult. On the contrary, I have assumed throughout this book that your clients are intelligent, sophisticated people. If someone is intelligent and sophisticated, you can be sure that they'd rather be applying those qualities to managing their own business, not to wearing themselves out ploughing through your proposal.

Make your proposal easy to read and your readers will reward you. This chapter introduces the principles of reader-friendly writing, as applied to proposals.

Write for the reader, not for yourself

All proposals have one thing in common. They are written to help the reader. They must show how the reader will benefit, and help them come to the 'right' decision (i.e. to use your services). This may sound obvious, but it's important to bear in mind with every word you write. Sometimes, especially if you have thought of a really interesting set of ideas, it is easy to become carried away with your own inventiveness and the elegance of the solution. If you forget to show how your solution meets the reader's needs, however, you will lose them in the first few paragraphs.

In a sense you have to 'sell' your reader the proposal itself before you can sell the ideas within it. If the proposal does not provide a good service in terms of organization and readability you are off to a bad start. If, on the other hand, the proposal is well-organized and easy to read, your readers will be more receptive to your ideas.

Please care about your readers. Think about them all the time. Ask yourself:

- What do they want?
- What do they need?
- What do they care about?
- What makes them enthusiastic?
- What turns them off?

Tailor the structure and wording of your proposal with the same attention to detail that you would apply to the actual project.

Remember that people may be reading your proposal for different reasons. For example, they may read it because:

- They asked you to write it.
- It's their job to read it.
- They need the information.
- You made them want to read it.

Only the last of these factors is within your control. Reading your proposal should be a painless and even pleasurable experience.

The more you know about your readers, the better equipped you are to write a proposal that works. Writing for the reader means structuring your proposal to suit the way that they *will* read it, not the way you think they *should* read it. It means using the language they feel most comfortable with. It means not blinding them with science if they are not scientists, but giving the technocrats the details they want. Writing to suit your reader takes just a little more effort than writing to suit yourself, but it will more than repay that effort by increasing your chances of success.

Don't assume that your proposal will be read from cover to cover

It might be nice to think that after you have lavished your time and care on every section of the proposal, it will be read from cover to cover. This just doesn't happen. Hardly anyone reads a proposal like a novel; it will probably be read more like a newspaper. People will flick back and forth through the proposal looking for the parts that interest them. A technical expert might dive straight into the technical detail. A purchasing manager might turn straight to the back to find the price.

There's nothing wrong with this approach – after all, you almost certainly do it yourself. So, be kind to your readers, and pander to their butterfly minds. It makes sense to structure your proposal so that readers can find the sections they want without the frustration of having to wade through a lot of other text they may see as irrelevant.

Don't assume that everyone will read every section

Not everyone will read your proposal in the order you write it but, just as important, some people will read only one or two sections. Again, don't see this as a slur on your efforts – it just reflects the different needs of your customers. However, you should cater for these needs by organizing your material in a reader-friendly way.

For example, always include a concise, readable summary. This might be the only part that the managing director will read before signing-off a decision made by a departmental manager.

You should also make clear distinctions between sections. For example, if your proposal contains a section on implications for the client's computer network, this must be clearly distinguished so that the IT manager can find it and see how the IT department will be affected. If the pricing section is the only one that the purchasing manager will read, you might include two or three lines repeating exactly what they are about to buy, and when it will be delivered. Repetition, yes, but as we shall see, repetition can occasionally be constructive.

Don't assume that any of your readers will take in everything they read

Research shows that most people don't take in everything the first time that they read it. How many times has a client or colleague asked you a question that you know is answered in full in the document they have just read? For that matter, how often have *you* asked someone a question only to be told 'but it's all explained in the memo. Haven't you read it?'

People are not being difficult or rude when they do this. They genuinely think they *have* studied the document in detail. But, in fact, their eyes have been skipping over the sentences and paragraphs, picking up on the words and phrases that catch their eye. The brain tends to fill in the gaps, so they *think* they know what they have read.

It's rather like the well-known demonstration of the unreliability of witnesses. Three people are asked to watch a short film of a robbery, then asked later to describe what happened. They will all give a coherent description of the events, but they won't all give the same description. The versions of events will vary quite markedly – one witness might say there were three men involved, another four. One will say the ringleader had a gun, another that he had a baseball bat.

It's the same with reading. People take in part of what they read and fill in the gaps for themselves. The situation worsens if they are reading in the normal office situation – the phone's ringing, constant interruptions, a million and one other things to do.

Don't despair. There are ways in which you can combat the natural tendency for readers to miss important points.

- *Come straight to the point.* Beginnings usually command attention, so put your most important messages in prime positions – at the start of sections or paragraphs, even at the start of sentences.
- *Headings, lists and bullet points attract attention.* They can be used to highlight key points, shouting out loudly:

Read me, I am important.

- *Repetition increases your chances of being read.* Repeating key points in strategic positions will ensure that even the most inattentive reader stands a fair chance of picking up the message. It's not enough to state the key benefits to the client once – they might be missed. Find ways of repeating them, perhaps changing the wording for variety.

Don't be afraid that readers will complain about the repetition. Oddly enough, clients never tire of hearing about what *they* are going to get out of the project. It's when you keep repeating trite phrases about how wonderful *you* are, or boring technical details, that repetition becomes annoying.

Don't assume that all your readers are experts

Proposals about technical subjects will contain a great deal of technical detail, which is fine for any technical experts who may be reading it. Remember, however, that your proposal may be read by all sorts of people once it is out of your hands. You have no knowledge or control over what happens to the proposal once it leaves your desk. Thus it makes sense to be kind to the non-expert reader by writing in a way that they can understand. You can help them by providing:

- a jargon-free summary
- a background section – invaluable for the non-expert – which the technically-oriented reader will be able to skip
- a table of abbreviations
- a glossary of technical terms as an appendix.

In the following chapters, we'll be considering some of the specific techniques you can use to ensure that your proposal gets its message across in spite of – or because of – reader behaviour.

Summary

- Write for the reader, not for yourself.

- Don't assume that your proposal will be read from cover to cover.

- Don't assume that everyone will read every section.

- Don't assume that any of your readers will take in everything they read.

- Don't assume that all your readers are experts.

Action points

1. Study a proposal that you're currently writing, or a recent example. List all the people in the client company who are likely to read it. Note who are the main decision makers and influencers. Now examine the structure and content of your proposal.

   - Are you sure that all readers will be able to find the information they need, quickly and easily?
   - Have you provided necessary background information for non-technical readers (clearly identified so that technical readers do not feel they are being talked down to)?
   - Have you repeated your key client benefits in at least three different places to make sure the reader cannot escape seeing them (e.g. in the covering letter, the summary and the body text)?

6   Clear writing

If there is one quality that characterizes a good business writing style, it is clarity. To communicate your message you must first clarify your meaning.

Clarity in business writing comes from three main sources:

- good organization (see Chapters 3 and 4)
- short, simple sentences and paragraphs
- choice of words that everyone will understand.

Sounds simple? In one way it is. Consider a ten-year-old's description of a day out. It will be clear, vivid and direct, with no convoluted sentences, abstract concepts, meaningless jargon or clichés.

> Yesterday we went to Alton Towers. We went in the minibus with Mrs Scott. Darren was sick. We had a great time.

As we grow up we learn to express more complex ideas in a more complex way. There is nothing wrong with that. However, many of us go a step further. We learn to express simple ideas in a complex way. This is not so good. We begin to copy styles of writing that we find in books. We receive advice from teachers, parents and colleagues. Sadly, many of the models that we copy are based on outmoded styles of expression – so old-fashioned they evoke the Victorian age of 'I remain, sir, your most humble and obedient servant'.

By the time we have been through secondary or higher education and become business writers, most of us have acquired a heavy veneer of 'respectability' in our prose. Sometimes this veneer is so thick it is hard to see the ideas underneath. We have lost the clarity that comes with simplicity.

Too much business writing is needlessly fussy, complicated and pompous. It is a strain to read and understand. It is an insult to the reader, your client. If your client has a superior intellect, why should he or she want to apply it to deciphering your efforts? Clear writing is client-friendly – it is one of the ways in which you give your clients the best possible service.

This chapter looks at the basic skills you need to get your message across loud and clear. The great authority on the English language, H.W. Fowler, said that we should strive for writing that is 'direct, simple, brief, vigorous and lucid'. What better qualities could you ask for in a proposal? Here's how to achieve them.

Write in your natural voice

Few people are naturally convoluted or pompous in their speech, but far more are complicated and affected in their writing. One of the easiest ways to make your writing read more clearly is to write in your natural voice. Use the kinds of words and phrases you would use when talking to the client, or giving a sales presentation.

Most people wouldn't say to the client: 'It is our considered opinion that it would be advantageous for Billings Buttons to undertake a fully comprehensive review of its manufacturing methodologies'. You would be much more likely to say something like 'We recommend that Billings Buttons should review the whole of its manufacturing process'. So why insist on writing the more complicated and wordy version?

Good business writing flows naturally, like speech, but all the 'ums' and 'ers', slang and unnecessary repetition are taken out. If you can write with your natural voice, instead of trying to acquire someone else's, then you will write more quickly and easily. Of course if you are one of the rare individuals who *do* speak like the first example above, you will probably have to seek the help of a kind colleague to demystify your prose.

Don't be afraid to use short words

Most business writers have a habit of thoughtlessly using long words to perform simple everyday tasks. Many people feel that it is more polite or formal to use long words instead of their everyday equivalents – 'approximately' instead of 'about', 'advantageous' instead of 'helpful', 'endeavour' instead of 'try'. Long words are seen as lending an air of seriousness and importance.

There are some historical reasons for this. Long words in English are usually derived from Latin or Greek, whereas their shorter equivalents are usually of Anglo-Saxon origin. Latin was once the international language of scholarship, and the Latin-based language French was, for a time, the polite language of the English nobility. Long Latin-based words have therefore been used for centuries to convey a kind of class distinction in English.

This need not concern us too much today. The short, familiar word has some heavyweight supporters among experts on the use of English. Sir Ernest Gowers in *The Complete Plain Words* says: 'Be short, be simple, be human'. H.W. Fowler in *Modern English Usage* says: 'Prefer the short word to the long'. George Orwell in *Politics and the English Language* says: 'Never use a long word where a short word will do'.

Short words are easier to read and understand than long words and will communicate your meaning more quickly. In contrast, long words are tiring to read. If your readers are unused to them they will feel threatened. If, as is more likely, they know what the word means, they may be annoyed or amused by your pretentiousness. A proposal is intended to sell your services, not to enable you to flaunt your vocabulary.

There are, however, two valid reasons for using long words in factual writing:

- to make your meaning more specific
- to avoid clumsy repetition.

For example, you might feel that it is more precise to use 'presentation' to describe the typical business situation in which a talk is given accompanied by slides or overhead transparencies. Everyone recognizes the specific meaning of 'presentation' in business. 'Talk' or 'speech' would be shorter but would convey your meaning less effectively.

If you started with '*After* the new recruits have attended the induction course they will receive customer service training', you might prefer to go on to say '*Following* this they will spend a week in each department of the store, *after* which they will be given their first jobs'. Even though 'following' is longer, it adds variety.

If we took the 'short words' advice to the extreme, our writing might read like a series of grunts and snorts. There's little chance of this happening because most people already lean too far in the other direction – that of using long words which add no extra meaning.

The following list contains some of the most common culprits and their shorter alternatives. If you can substitute the shorter word, say 70 per cent of the time, you will have taken an important step towards making your writing clearer and more pleasant to read.

Instead of	why not use
purchase or acquire	buy
quantify	measure
communicate	write/speak
approximately	about
following	after
permit	let
however	but
utilize	use
manufacture	make

sufficient	enough
demonstrate	show
necessity	need
accordingly	so
advantageous	helpful
concerning	about
discontinue	stop
endeavour	try
evident	clear
location	place
magnitude	size
regarding	about
remainder	rest
request	ask
requirement	need
subsequent	next

Cut out unnecessary words

With the 'long words' habit goes the 'wordy phrases' habit. Unlike long words, which sometimes have their place, wordiness is never justified. George Orwell advised writers: 'If a word can be cut, cut it'. Eradicate wordy phrases ruthlessly from your writing – they make you look pompous and obscure your message.

Here are a few of the commonest offending phrases. If this is one of your writing problems, compile your own list and practise eradicating them from your work.

Avoid	**and use**
as a means of	to
ask the question	ask
at the present time	now
during the time that	while
in order that	so that
with regard to	about
prior to	before
with the exception of	except for

a considerable number of	many
at a rapid rate	rapidly/quickly
a certain amount of	some
for the reason that	because
referred to as	called
at an early date	soon
in view of the fact that	because/since
during the course of	during/while

Smothered verbs

You will often see a particular kind of wordy phrase called a 'smothered verb'. A verb is smothered by turning it into a noun and adding another verb like 'make', 'give', 'take' or 'come'. The result is a phrase such as 'come to a decision' when all you needed to say was 'decide'. Watch out for smothered verbs and edit them ruthlessly from your proposals.

Here are a few examples:

Instead of	**use**
make a decision	decide
come to the realization	realize
take into/under consideration	consider
make an estimate	estimate
give an explanation	explain
make a presentation of	present
is indicative of/is an indication of	indicates
place an emphasis on	emphasize
come to a conclusion	conclude
undertake an investigation	investigate
give a description of	describe

An exception – when to use several words where one will do

There is one circumstance when you may want to use several words even though there is a single word which means the same thing. This is when the single word is unfamiliar, confusing, or a jargon word that only a few of your audience will understand.

Thus, you might want to say that the market is 'dominated by a few powerful companies' instead of saying that it is an 'oligopoly'; or that an employment policy is 'likely to lead to resentment' instead of that it is 'invidious'.

Avoid redundancy

A last word on wordiness – avoid redundancy. There is a temptation to emphasize your point by saying that something is 'absolutely true' or 'fully complete'. Either it is true or complete, or it is not. To help you to avoid falling into this trap, here are a few redundant phrases you may see in everyday business writing:

Instead of	use
absolutely complete	complete
completely finished	finished
try and endeavour	try
meet with	meet
true facts	facts
advance plan	plan
basic essentials	basics *or* essentials
current status	status
estimate approximately	estimate
past history	history
large in size	large
few in number	few

Activate your verbs

Using the active voice is one of the most effective improvements you can make to your business writing. What does this mean? It's simple. When the active voice is used, the subject of the sentence performs an action. The subject is the 'doer'. For example:

The boy threw the ball.
Sally wrote the proposal.
The Research Department has analysed the results of the survey.

Contrast this with the passive voice, in which the subject is acted upon:

> The ball was thrown by the boy.
> The proposal was written by Sally.
> The results of the survey have been analysed by the Research Department.

You will notice two things about the passive voice:

- it uses more words to say exactly the same thing
- it usually sounds duller.

It pays to go through your writing carefully and see if you can increase your use of the active voice. Some word-processing programs and grammar checkers will estimate the percentage of sentences written in the passive voice. The acceptable level of passive constructions varies with the tone you are trying to achieve. For example, a newspaper story will be written almost entirely in the active voice because journalists know that is what best conveys the message. In contrast, a paper in a learned scientific journal will usually contain a high proportion of passive constructions.

Most business writers use far more passive constructions than are necessary or desirable. While the percentage of passive constructions tends to rise with the formality of the tone, it is still possible to be very formal and correct while using the active voice.

This sentence written in the active voice:

> Geological studies have shown that the Holywell site is unsuitable for the storage of contaminated waste.

is clearer and more concise, but no less serious or formal, than the two following passive constructions:

> The Holywell site has been shown by geological studies to be unsuitable for the storage of contaminated waste.
> It has been shown by geological studies that the Holywell site is unsuitable for the storage of contaminated waste.

The first example also demonstrates an important point – the active voice does not have to be used with proper names or the first person. It is often assumed that you cannot use the active voice unless you say 'we' or 'I' or 'Sally' or 'Harry'. This is not the case. However, you should not be afraid to use 'we' or even 'I' in moderation in your proposals.

It is often better to say:

We have assessed the existing management structure.

rather than …

The existing management structure has been assessed.

After all, you're not ashamed of the fact that your company performed the assessment, in fact you're rather proud of it.

There are three situations in which the passive voice is preferable to the active voice:

- If the performer of the action is unknown or unimportant. 'The factory was built in 1986.' You can hardly say: 'Some builders built the factory in 1986'.
- If you want to emphasize the object of the sentence (the person or thing that is being acted upon). 'This unique process was patented by ICI' might be better than 'ICI patented this unique process' if you are going on to talk about the unique process and what it will do for the customer.
- If you would rather not say who performed the action. 'The cost of the project was underestimated.' Let us hope that the occasions on which you wish to avoid responsibility are few.

Use short sentences

It is often said that a sentence should contain a single thought. If you start a new thought, start a new sentence. Of course the length of a thought is rather difficult to define. Here are some practical guidelines on sentence length.

Often, the average sentence length in a business document is about 30–40 words, such as the following:

> Long sentences are exhausting and confusing for the reader, as they are difficult to follow, and unless the reader is concentrating very hard, and paying close attention to what you have to say, they may lose their concentration halfway through and only understand part of the message.

If you want to keep your readers with you, limit the length of your sentences. For comfortable reading, most sentences should be 20 words or less. This applies even to a sophisticated well-educated audience – if you check the 'quality' newspapers you will find that most sentences in the news articles are less than 20 words. Use even shorter sentences if you are writing for people whose first language is not English.

A 30-word sentence should be a rarity. If you do use a long sentence, punctuate it carefully and make sure that it is carefully constructed to make the meaning clear. If you have written more than three subordinate clauses in a sentence, or more than four punctuation marks, it's probably too long. Try splitting it into two sentences.

Do not hesitate to use very short sentences where they come naturally – their shortness can make them stand out and drive home your message. An eight word sentence is easy to read. Like short words, the short sentence tends to be despised by people who think their ideas are too complex to be expressed in everyday language. In fact, very complex ideas can sometimes be encapsulated in very short sentences – 'God is love' or 'Less is more'.

On a less philosophical note, try to vary your sentence length. A piece of text consisting entirely of 20-word sentences would have a soporific effect, whereas a piece composed entirely of 8-word sentences would read like machine-gun fire. A mixture creates a pleasant rhythmical effect.

If you never use several words to do the work of one, you will already be well on the way to writing shorter sentences. You can also break up long sentences into two or more shorter sentences. Even if this means adding a word or two, the beneficial effect on the readability of your writing will be worthwhile.

If we use shorter words, shorter sentences and avoid unnecessary wordiness, our writing becomes much clearer. For example:

> It is our recommendation that the canteen facilities in Westalls Ltd be replaced by a fast-food outlet, thereby implementing a substantial reduction in expenditure on canteen wages, and the cost of gas and electricity supplies. In addition, this measure will offer an additional source of income, as a proportion of those employees who formerly patronized Mr Chippy will then be inclined to purchase their lunches on site.

could be replaced by ...

> We recommend that the Westalls canteen be replaced by a fast-food outlet. This will reduce costs for wages, gas and electricity. It will also increase income, as some employees who previously used Mr Chippy will now buy their lunches on site.

Can you see where the changes have been made, without losing information or changing the level of formality?

Use plenty of paragraphs

Paragraphs have two functions:

- to group related thoughts
- to provide visual relief.

If a sentence can be thought of as a single thought, a paragraph is a string of related thoughts. When you change the direction of your thoughts, start a new paragraph. You can usually marshal your related thoughts into groups of 2–5 sentences. Business writers often use too few paragraphs because they have not grouped their thoughts sufficiently logically – they tend to meander on from one subject to another. If you have mentally done all the sorting and classifying of your facts, ideas and arguments, however, you will find that your text falls naturally into short paragraphs.

You were probably taught at school that a paragraph must consist of at least two sentences. In fact there may be times when you have a one-sentence thought and want to attract the reader's attention.

You can use a one-sentence paragraph occasionally, for emphasis.

It is often best to make your logic clear to the reader by beginning with a general statement that indicates what is coming in the rest of the paragraph. This is called a 'topic sentence'. For example:

Taking on new sales staff is a difficult business decision. [topic sentence] You may need the extra capacity now in order to expand. But you may be concerned about what will happen if the market changes over the next couple of years. Will you be faced with the trauma and expense of redundancies?

Contract representatives could be the answer to your problem. [topic sentence] Well-trained and well-disciplined, they can work alongside your permanent sales force for as long as they are needed. You have the option to renew the contract – and the option to decline if your needs change.

Make it flow with 'linking' words and phrases

You can help make your writing clearer by showing the connections between sentences and paragraphs with 'linking' words and phrases. For example:

When you add one point to another
'and', 'in addition', 'moreover', 'furthermore'

When indicating similarity
'likewise', 'similarly', 'in the same way'

When contrasting
'but', 'in contrast', 'however', 'on the contrary', 'on the other hand', 'nevertheless', 'although', 'even so', 'in spite of/despite'

When showing how one thing results from another
'so', 'therefore', 'hence', 'thus', 'as a result', 'consequently', 'accordingly'

When summing up
'in conclusion', 'in summary', 'to summarize', 'to conclude', 'in brief', 'in other words'

Judicious use of these words and phrases can tie your ideas together and make your writing flow. But remember that there is nothing wrong with the shorter ones. For example, try 'but' and 'so' where you might otherwise use 'however' or 'therefore'. See Chapter 10 for a discussion of whether you can start a sentence with 'but' – the short answer is that it is acceptable to most experts in the use of English, but may not be liked by some of your readers.

Use parallel structures

Parallel structures – series of word groups or whole sentences with the same kind of structure – add clarity and appeal to the reader's need to see order in your writing.
    For example, there is nothing wrong with:

The campaign will encourage people to eat healthily, exercise regularly and keep their drinking within sensible limits.

But this version is more readable, because it uses parallel verbs and adjectives. Nothing important is lost.

The campaign will encourage people to eat healthily, exercise regularly and drink sensibly.

Parallel structures are particularly important in lists:

Why offer stress counselling to your managers? An executive's performance can be affected by stress-related problems such as:

- they feel tired all the time
- losing concentration when at work
- depression and anxiety
- some suffer headaches and digestive problems
- irritability and anger.

This would read much more smoothly if it was 'tidied' into groups of nouns like this:

Why offer stress counselling to your managers? An executive's performance can be affected by stress-related problems such as:

- tiredness
- loss of concentration
- depression and anxiety
- headaches and digestive problems
- irritability and anger.

It could be expanded to include more information, in cause-and-effect pairs:

Why offer stress counselling to your managers? An executive's performance can be affected by stress-related problems. For example:

- *Tiredness* results in poor motivation
- *Loss of concentration* results in unnecessary mistakes
- *Depression and anxiety* lead to absenteeism
- *Headaches and digestive problems* mean time 'off sick'
- *Irritability and anger* alienate colleagues.

Write about people, things and facts

George Orwell tells us that we should 'Prefer the concrete to the abstract'. In other words we should write about people, things and facts, wherever possible, instead of about ideas. Wherever possible your readers should be able to visualize what is going to happen. This not only makes your proposal easier to understand, it also makes it more convincing. If readers can see something in their mind's eye, they are more likely to believe that it will happen.

I would much rather 'write a book' than 'develop an information resource'. (Notice how the concrete can also be less pompous than the abstract.)

You could say:

> An investigation will be conducted of the current procedures regarding the disposal of contaminated wastes at installations in the northern sector.

But why not say:

> John Smith will visit the Huddersfield and Bury sites, and interview managers, supervisors and plant workers to find out how they dispose of contaminated wastes.

The second version is only three words longer, yet it manages to say who is going to do the job, how they will do it, and where they will do it (complete, of course, with active sentence constructions). Isn't that more convincing to a potential client?

Summary

- Write with your natural voice.

- Don't be afraid to use short sentences, short words and short paragraphs.

- Cut out unnecessary words.

- Avoid jargon your readers won't understand.

- Use the active voice wherever you can.

- Use parallel structures, especially in lists.

- Write about people, things and facts.

Action points

1 Calculate the readability score of your latest proposal. This score (also known as a fog index) gives a crude measure of the readability of your writing, based on sentence length and the number of long words. You may find that your word processor's grammar-checking program calculates a readability score automatically. If not, here's how to do it:

   - Select a passage of about 100 words ending in a full stop.
   - Work out the average sentence length (total number of words divided by number of sentences).
   - Count the number of words with three syllables or more, like 'plen | ti | tude' (three syllables), 're | pet | it | ion' (four syllables), or 'pre | cip | it | a | tion' (five syllables). BUT do not count true technical terms (e.g. 'carburettor'), proper nouns (e.g. 'President', 'Liverpool') and two-syllable words that have been made into three-syllable words by adding a plural ending, or -ed, or -ing (e.g. 'transported', 'pedalling').
   - Work out the percentage of 'difficult' words (three or more syllables).
   - Add the percentage of difficult words to the average sentence length.
   - Multiply by 0.4.

   This gives you the readability score, which is roughly equivalent to the reading age score used for testing school-children. However, don't be misled – if you have a score of 32, that doesn't mean that anyone over 32 can read it! In practice, any writing with a readability score over 18 is likely to be very hard work for even the most educated reader. What is more, you can't assume that all your readers will be educated to a high level, or be native English speakers.

   Research shows that readers are most comfortable with writing that is below their maximum reading age. Business writers should aim for a readability score of no more than 14–16 – less than this is perfectly acceptable.

Don't be afraid that writing to this level will make your proposal sound childish. It won't. Many famous authors, such as Ernest Hemingway and Kingsley Amis, consistently score below 12, as do most stories in the popular daily newspapers. Even the 'quality' newspapers rarely score more than 16, and complex articles in scientific journals *can* score as low as 14 if they are carefully written.

2   Read through a three-page section of your proposal (continuous text, not lists or tables). Highlight every sentence in which you have used the passive voice. How many of these sentences could be improved by changing to the active?

3   Read through again this time highlighting the key sentences (those that introduce or encapsulate vital facts or ideas).

   – Try the 'topic sentence test'. Do most key sentences come at the beginnings of paragraphs, not buried in the middle (i.e. are you using topic sentences to focus the reader's attention)?
   – Try the 'waffle test'.[1] Is there a fairly even distribution of key sentences (i.e. sentences that make important points) throughout the text? If the key sentences are all bunched together in one place, you will probably find you are 'waffling' in the sections in which no key sentences occur.

---

1   I am indebted to medical journalist Tim Albert for this diagnostic technique.

7 Powerful writing

If your writing is well organized, client-friendly and clear, you will already have gone a long way towards selling your ideas. However, there is still more that you can do to increase the selling power of your proposal.

You can use specific techniques to add persuasive power to your writing. These techniques are not difficult to learn and can be very effective. Once explained they will seem familiar to you, because many of them are also used by copywriters in consumer advertising. A proposal isn't the same as an advertisement, but that doesn't mean that you can't borrow some of the techniques and modify them to suit your own style.

Choose the right tone

Like speech, writing has a tone. The difference between tone in writing and tone in conversation is that writing is a one-way communication. If you are talking to someone face-to-face, you make conscious or unconscious adjustments in tone all the time, as you gauge their reaction to your words, gestures and body language.

In writing, such fine-tuning is impossible. You have to choose a tone and stick with it. You do not have the option to make subtle adjustments based on your audience's response. This lack of instant reaction is one of the factors that makes people feel uncomfortable about putting their ideas in writing. If you have well developed interpersonal skills, you will be well aware of the harm that can be done to your case by being too informal with someone who is a stickler for protocol, or too stiff when your client is naturally easy-going and 'laid back'.

Here are some tips to help you choose the right tone for your proposal.

Consider the business culture (the client's and your own)

A traditional conservative business demands a traditional conservative tone. If you are writing for a fast-moving trendsetting business, you can write in a more 'zappy' informal way. Thus, for a firm of City of London solicitors, you might choose to say:

> 'Unless carefully managed, the relocation of a company can be highly disruptive for the business, and damaging to staff morale. As relocation experts we can help you to minimize these problems.'

If you were writing for an advertising agency, you might prefer a more informal tone:

> 'Anyone who has ever moved house knows what a nightmare it can be. It's even worse when you move a company. Your business suffers. Your staff suffer. As relocation experts, we can help ease the pain.'

The culture of *your* company is also important, because the tone creates a picture of what you are like. For example, a firm of accountants would probably prefer to use a restrained formal tone, in keeping with what is expected of their calling. Even if they *were* proposing to an advertising agency, they would still be formal, because that is what the client would expect of them.

Consider the national culture

If you are writing for readers in another country, think about the level of formality in business dealings. If you are writing for a

Japanese or German company, for example, you will probably need to be more formal than if you were writing for Australians or Scandinavians.

If in doubt, err on the side of formality (not pomposity)

You can never be sure who is going to read your proposal, or what their prejudices will be. More people are likely to be offended by inappropriate informality than by too stiff a tone. Try to cater for the 'top end' of the formality scale for your particular client.

But remember that formality should never mean pomposity. You can be formal without giving way to the wordiness and convoluted expressions that characterize pompous writing. There are often good reasons to be formal, but there is never a good reason to be pompous.

Take your tone from the client

Imagine you were meeting the client. Would you chat away easily, or would you converse in a more structured, formal way? Would you call them by their first name? Would your meetings have a written agenda and be formally chaired? The level of formality you have experienced in person will act as a guide to what is expected in writing.

Where there is a written brief or other documents from the client, follow their tone. If they are very formal, you should be likewise. If they use friendly colloquial language, so should you.

Be positive

Whatever the level of formality your writing should always convey the impression that you know what you are doing, that the project will go according to plan and that, if there are any problems, you are confident of your ability to solve them. If your writing makes you appear tentative or equivocal, the client is likely to feel uneasy about your recommendations and your company.

There are two specific techniques for creating the positive, confident image that will help you to sell:

- Don't hedge if you can avoid it.
- Turn negatives into positives.

Don't hedge if you can avoid it

'Hedging' is the way in which we cover ourselves against being wrong. We choose words that indicate uncertainty such as 'may be', 'could be', 'should be', 'possibly' and 'probably'. Hedging has its place where we really are uncertain – the problem is, we often indicate uncertainty when we don't mean to.

For example, in technical writing it would be perfectly appropriate to say:

> The evidence *suggests* that the bridge *may* have collapsed owing to faulty construction.

This raises a possibility, but no more. If you wanted to be a little more definite, but still avoid committing yourself you might say:

> The evidence *suggests* that the bridge collapsed owing to faulty construction.

Only if you were absolutely sure would you state baldly:

> The bridge collapsed owing to faulty construction.

That's a perfectly legitimate use of hedging. But in business we often hedge when we do not mean or need to. You could say:

> Her CV *suggests* that she *may* be a useful addition to the marketing team.

But you would be better off with:

> Her CV *suggests* that she *will* be a useful addition to the marketing team.

In fact, you might (notice I'm hedging here!) only need to say:

> She *will* be a useful addition to the marketing team.

This example of hedging shows it as just a mild distraction, introducing unnecessary wordiness and vagueness. But when used in proposals, hedging can have a pronounced negative effect.

As a client, would you rather be told this:

> The first phase *should be* completed within four working weeks.

or this?

> The first phase *will be* completed within four working weeks.

The second version shows more conviction and commitment, which is exactly the impression you want to convey. Now, you might argue that you cannot guarantee that the first phase will be completed within four working weeks, because some factors might be outside your control. But you can always follow up by stating what your estimate is based on, which you would need to do even if you used the 'should be' format. You have nothing to lose by being more definite about when the first phase will be completed.

Let's take another example. Which shows more conviction, this …

> Using a single supplier *can be expected to* cut costs.

or this?

> Using a single supplier *will* cut costs.

If you use the stronger second version, who is going to argue with you? And if they did, couldn't you put up a strong defence of your point of view? The point about the 'avoid hedging' rule of positive writing is not that you should make unjustifiable statements – you shouldn't – but that you can make strong positive statements if you are in a position to back them up.

Turn negatives into positives

There are people (usually the ones with a fixed smile and a slightly mad look in their eyes) who will tell you that 'you can always turn a negative into a positive'. They mean in life, but the same principle also applies in writing. Often, you can turn a statement that might be perceived as bad news into good news. Rather than tell the client what *can't* be done, sometimes it's better to tell them what *can* be done, and leave the can't to their imagination.

Thus:

> Without the full support of management in the subsidiaries, it may be difficult to complete the project successfully.

could become:

> The full support of management in the subsidiaries will ensure the success of the project.

Similarly, this is a rather downbeat way of putting what could be a very important selling point:

> We feel it is very important to have experience in implementation as well as strategy, because without the knowledge of implementation, strategies can be impractical and unworkable.

Wouldn't it be more effective to reword it something like this, and say what you really mean?

> Our experience in implementation as well as strategy will ensure that the advice we give is not only imaginative, but practical and workable.

Increasing the strength of the wording just a little, without telling any lies, can sometimes help to give the positive 'feel' that you need.

For example, this could sound a little weak:

> We have undertaken several projects for other clients similar to the range of work we are recommending to you in this proposal.

How many is 'several'? If it is an impressive number, use it (see 'Be specific', below). If you chose 'several' because you really mean 'we've done a few projects that were a little bit like this', you could rewrite the message to sound more positive, while not telling any untruths:

> Our solid experience gained with previous similar projects gives us a clear insight into your needs.

Notice that in this last example you have introduced something new – why your experience (paltry though it may be) is relevant to the client. *In other words, you have told them a benefit.* Which brings us to a crucial piece of advice.

Stress the benefits, not the features

It's a rare client who is interested simply in the beauty of your product or service. They want to know what it will do for them. In other words, they are more interested in the benefits than the features. The question uppermost in their minds is 'What's in it for me?' Or to paraphrase John Kennedy, 'Ask not what you can do, ask what you can do for your customer.' A feature can be a physical attribute of your product, a point in the schedule, or the experience of people in the firm. Refer back to your needs analysis – this will help you to determine what benefits the customer would like to see.

Never assume that the customer can infer the benefit from the feature. What if they are not familiar with the technical area? What if they are simply not paying close attention? What if your competitors are driving home the benefits with a sledgehammer?

In proposal writing, as with most aspects of communication, it never hurts to state the obvious. It may be obvious to you, but you can't assume that it's obvious to everyone. If it's important, put it in writing. Nowhere is this more true than with benefits – one of the most important parts of your proposal.

Feature:

> We have more extensive pensions management experience than any other UK firm.

Benefit:

The smooth running of your pension scheme will be assured by our extensive experience, the greatest of any firm in the UK.

Feature:

Our staff have been trained to exceptionally high standards.

Benefit:

Your queries will be answered quickly and accurately by our highly trained staff.

Feature:

The system will produce weekly or monthly stock updates.

Benefit:

To help you keep track of your stock, the system will automatically produce weekly or monthly reports.

or even better ...

Benefit plus explanation:

Good stock control can save you thousands of pounds in interest payments each year. To help you keep track of your stock, the system will automatically produce weekly or monthly reports.

This last example brings out another important point. Sometimes the customer may need to see the benefit spelt out in detail. This is especially true if you have identified a need that they have not thought out clearly by themselves. Not everyone in the company may be aware of the financial benefits of good stock control. If yours is the proposal that gets this message across, you will have a competitive advantage.

Note that you do not necessarily have to use the word 'benefit' to communicate your message. Directly or indirectly, you will be talking about them throughout the proposal, so saying 'the benefits to Smith's Industries will be … ' could become repetitive. You might like to ring the changes with alternatives such as:

advantage
gain
profit
value
worth
merit
significance
consequence
implication
meaning
relevance
effect
outcome
result
impact

Make it real

Readers relate better to people, facts and things, than they do to abstract ideas. You want your readers to picture exactly what they are getting in terms of the product or service. This will build client confidence in your organization.

There are two ways in which you can create this sense of reality:

- Be as specific as possible.
- Use examples and case histories to illustrate key points.

Be specific
When describing what the reader will receive for their money, be as precise and informative as possible.

For example, why say 'regular progress checks', when you can say something much more specific, such as 'daily computerized project monitoring'?

Likewise, why say 'The new process will cut wastage substantially', if you are able to say 'The new process will cut wastage by 20%'?

Why say 'We have completed similar projects for other companies in this field', when you can say 'We have completed five similar environmental audits for mining companies worldwide'?

Use examples and case histories to illustrate key points

Examples and case histories are another aspect of being specific. They help to give your ideas a sense of reality. The right example in the right place can do much to enhance your credibility.

Suppose you are interviewing someone for a job and you ask the question 'What would you do in such-and-such a situation?' Which candidate impresses you most? The one who says 'Well I suppose if that happened, I would have to do such-and-such ... '? Or the one who says 'Well, the last time I was placed in a situation like that was ... and what I did was ... '? Most people would find the second one more convincing.

You can see the proposal as a sort of job interview on paper. The interviewee (i.e. company) with a relevant, pithy example has a built-in advantage over the one who can only discuss a hypothetical situation.

There are two important types of example that the proposal can use:

- examples from past projects
- realistic projections.

Examples from past projects   This type of example includes everything from a one-liner to a complete case history.

Instead of saying:

> Our experience with similar projects means that we can ensure that even such a complex programme will run smoothly,

you might say:

> Our experience with similar projects means we can ensure that such a complex programme runs smoothly. For example, we always have at least two additional general speakers on standby in case one of the panellists is taken ill on the day of the conference.

Or you might give a case history to back up a claim:

> Our experience with similar projects means we can ensure that such a complex programme will run smoothly. For example, at a recent product launch for Grottomax Ltd, guest speaker Sir Gerald Hardly-Breathing of the Institute of Manufacturers was taken ill during lunch. Because we had an alternative speaker, Professor Charles Creditworthy of Barchester Business School, on standby, we were able to complete the launch without a hitch.

Realistic projections   Here you use your technical knowledge to make a realistic estimate of what your proposed plan will mean to the client.
For example:

> Our new call management system will cut your telephone bills by about 15%. For a company currently paying £15,000 each year, that means a saving of more than £2000.

> Using structured design techniques, the new software will be designed, tested and installed within 6 months. If work starts at the beginning of February, the system will be up and running by the beginning of August, in good time for the winter season.

Shift the emphasis to the reader

If you keep the reader's needs in mind, and emphasize benefits rather than features, then you will have gone a long way towards shifting the emphasis to the reader. But there are two other specific techniques you can use to make the reader feel that the proposal is 'just for them':

- use 'you' language.
- use the client's company name.

You will notice that much of this book is written in 'you' language because I am talking to you, the reader. I may not know your names as individuals, but I know that it's you I am trying to reach. The same approach can apply to proposals.

Not:

Changing to Filtroco could halve filtration costs over the next two years.

but:

Changing to Filtroco could halve *your* filtration costs over the next two years.

or, being positive:

Changing to Filtroco *will* halve your filtration costs over the next two years.

However, a proposal full of 'yous' would still not be quite right. For variety, use the company name. It's all too common to see proposals in which the name of the supplier seems to appear in every other sentence, but the name of the client does not appear at all. A more client-friendly image is achieved when the client's name is used at least as often as the supplier's name:

Changing to Filtroco will halve *Aquifer*'s filtration costs over the next two years.

Show conviction

When you are in the business of giving advice, you will want to use phrases like 'We recommend so and so … ' Bear in mind that some of these phrases are more powerful than others.

Most powerful: 'We believe', 'We recommend', 'We advise' and 'We counsel'.

Less powerful: 'In our opinion', 'We suggest', 'We think' and 'We feel'.

Choose the words that most accurately reflect the strength of your recommendation. Most proposals should have a preponderance of the stronger constructions, to show that you are convinced in your own mind about what you are recommending.

Incidentally, the passive construction 'It is recommended that' is not as powerful as the active construction 'We recommend' – if you are making the recommendation, take the responsibility. Who wants to follow a recommendation made by a person or persons unknown?

Use 'powerful' words

In advertising some of the words that are most likely to gain attention are:

you
money
save
new
now
results
easy
safe
discovery
proven
guaranteed
sex

Think about using these and other powerful words more often in your proposals (though I can't think where you would find the opportunity to use 'sex'). We are often so concerned with seeming professional that we avoid using the obvious potent words and prefer instead their watered-down equivalents.

You're not writing advertising copy, but that doesn't mean you can't usefully borrow some of the language that is used to sell cars and soap powder. Sophisticated readers are as susceptible to the power of emotive words as anyone else.

Instead of:

> Hypertext is a recently-introduced mechanism that allows readers to browse through large electronic documents,

how about:

> Hypertext is a new tool that will revolutionize the way we read documents on our office computers?

You will probably be able to think of words that seem to work magic in your own industry – such as:

cost-effectiveness
quality
teamwork
professionalism
leadership
customer focus
sustainable

But remember that, when overworked, many erstwhile 'power' words become clichés, for example 'innovative' has been so overused that it has largely lost its impact. If you're seeing a new buzzword all the time in business writing, it's usually only a matter of months before it starts to look tired.

Use the rule of three

For some reason people find groups of three particularly easy to remember. In many cultures three is also a magical or lucky number. Somehow we seem to be particularly comfortable with threes.

From time immemorial, public figures have used the 'rule of three' in their speeches. Julius Caesar: 'I came, I saw, I conquered.' Michael Heseltine: 'We will intervene before breakfast, before lunch, and before dinner.' Winston Churchill: 'I have nothing to offer but blood, sweat and tears.'

Did you notice anything odd about the last example? If you did, congratulations! Churchill actually said 'blood, toil, tears and sweat', but only a few people remember the 'toil,' because of the power of the rule of three.

The rule of three is also widely used in advertising: 'A Mars a day helps you work, rest and play'. And how many company names can you think of that are always represented by a three-letter abbreviation?

You might want to capitalize on the rule of three in your proposal. Could the key benefits of your proposal be grouped into three easily memorable categories, rather than dissipating their power by using a long list of minor points?

Summary

- Choose the right tone.

- Be positive:

  - avoid hedging
  - turn negatives into positives.

- Stress the benefits, not the features.

- Make it real:

  - be specific
  - use examples and case histories.

- Shift the emphasis to the reader:

  - use 'you' language
  - use the client's company name.

- Show conviction.

- Use 'powerful' words.

- Use the rule of three.

Action points

1 Take a section of a current or recent proposal, covering your recommendations to the client. Underline all the 'hedging' words, such as:

   may   might
   might   probably
   could   possibly
   should

   How many of the hedging words you have used are really necessary? Could you increase the strength of your sentences by eliminating some of them?

2 Examine closely:

   – the recommendations you have made to the client
   – the credentials of your company.

   Does every feature have an associated benefit? Apply the 'What's in it for me?' test to each feature.

3 Study the sections such as *Credentials* where you have made claims, e.g. 'extensive experience,' 'unrivalled knowledge,' 'old-established' and so on. What information have you provided to support these claims? Could you make them more plausible with specific information and examples? Can you link them with benefits to the client?

4 Take a three-page chunk of your proposal (again, the *Recommendations* or *Credentials* sections are best). Highlight the number of times you have used 'you' or the name of the client company. Now take a different colour and highlight the number of times you have used 'we' and your own company name. If references to you outnumber references to the client, think about ways in which you could shift the emphasis to the client.

8 Selling the people and the company

This chapter is about making the most of the CVs of your personnel and the expertise, experience and reputation of your company. Whatever the nature of your business, these proposal elements will usually play an important part in selling your services.

Individual and company credentials are particularly important when there is little to choose between you and your competitors in terms of the services you are offering. In some cases, such as when accountants or solicitors are pitching for a long-term relationship (the 'beauty parade'), they are the *only* specific feature on offer to the client. In other words, the 'beauty parade' proposal is almost all about explaining why you have the best people and the most effective organization.

Whatever the extent of these sections in your proposal, it pays to write them carefully. You can develop standardized templates, but, to be effective, they should be carefully selected and tailored to meet the needs of each project and each client.

Selling the people

First, the people. Clients are very aware of the fact that the quality of your team can be responsible for the success or failure of the project. The importance of this aspect of the proposal should never be underestimated. Some systems allot as many as *half* the technical marks for each proposal to personnel. Other organizations may not use such a formal scoring system, but they will be swayed in their decisions if they think you can offer a more experienced, more professional-sounding team than the competition.

CVs

The way to display the calibre of your team is through their CVs. It's important to *use* the selling opportunity that the CV offers. You are probably accustomed to the CVs used for job recruitment. Yet, this type of CV is hardly ever the most appropriate for a proposal. Why? Because it doesn't allow you to bring out the key selling points that will make the client *want* that person on their team.

Figure 8.1 is an example of how a typical 'job application' CV begins.

Having read it, are you still awake? Your client might well have dozed off. I've seen CVs in proposals that included details of where the consultant went to primary school, their children's names ... all sorts of information that is of no use to the client whatsoever and can only serve to irritate.

There are only three kinds of information that should be included in a proposal CV:

- recent experience relevant to the project, i.e. the information the client will be looking for
- important qualifications (i.e. post-school level) that will give the client a positive feeling about the person and their abilities
- special qualifications such as languages that may give you an advantage over the competition.

Written from this point of view, Susan Robinson's CV would look something like Figure 8.2.

Notice how much more relevant information has been packed into about the same space as the standard-size CV. Unlike the standard CV, all the information is relevant and is presented in order of likely interest to the client.

CURRICULUM VITAE

SUSAN ROBINSON

Address: 13 Collingham Gardens
                Greytown
                Lancs
                GR1 4EB
                Telephone: 045 654934

Date of birth: 22.11.54   Marital status: Divorced

Age: 41

Education

Cudlip Grammar School, Newcastle–upon–Tyne, 1965–72

'O' levels: French, German, Biology, Maths, English, History,
                Geography, Physics, Chemistry

'A' levels: Economics, Maths, Russian

University of Darlington, 1972–75

BA Hons (1st Class) Economics 1975
Captain Tiddlywinks Club 1973–1974

Figure 8.1   A job application CV — not suitable for a proposal

[Brief introduction telling the client who the person is and what role they will play in the project]

Dr Susan Robinson – Principal Consultant
Proposed Project Leader, Moldavian Restructuring Initiative
Dr Susan Robinson is a Principal Consultant with Hallforth Associates, and is one of our most experienced staff members, having been with us for more than ten years.

[Relevant experience, highlighting special skills]

Experience: Susan's recent assignments have included a year spent in Beltov, Ruritania (1993–94), where she acted as expert adviser to a Ruritanian Department of the Interior team developing new economic initiatives to replace the now collapsed steel industry. This assignment, jointly funded by the European Commission and the Ruritanian Government, made use not only of Susan's considerable experience in economic development, but also of her strong interpersonal skills. Her experience of working as a solo foreign advisor with an otherwise wholly Eastern European team, guiding and training them in the new methodologies for the market economy, will prove particularly useful in the Moldavian situation.

Other relevant assignments Susan has tackled for Hallforth Associates include a rural areas feasibility study for the Lithuanian Joint Restructuring Board and an analysis of potential sources of investment for small business development in Ruritania.

[Relevant qualifications]

Qualifications: Susan speaks fluent Russian, Ruritanian, and French, and is currently studying Moldavian. She has a first-class degree in Economics from the University of Darlington (1975), and a post-graduate Diploma in Planning from Forton Polytechnic (1976). Before joining Hallforth Associates, she worked in local government (Collingham District Council 1976–85), during which time she also studied for her PhD at Forton Polytechnic (The economic impact of inward investment by a Japanese electronics company on a small Northern town, 1985).

Figure 8.2   An effective proposal CV

General guidelines for presenting CVs in proposals can be summarized as follows:

- Keep it brief – no more than one side of A4; half a side is often enough.
- Give only relevant information.
- Give the information in order of interest to the client – relevant experience is usually of more interest than qualifications and should therefore go first.
- Degrees and post-graduate qualifications add prestige and should certainly be mentioned – school qualifications are rarely relevant and should usually be omitted.
- Personal details such as marital status and children should be left out unless specifically requested by the client. The person will be working as a consultant, not as an employee, and their personal circumstances should be of no concern. If personal circumstances *are* in any way relevant (e.g. for an overseas assignment), any necessary discussion with the client can take place *after* you have been awarded the contract.
- Don't expect the client to read between the lines. If a member of your staff is a world expert on something, say so! If the person in question is a modest individual who baulks at writing this sort of statement into their own CV, it's the job of the person overseeing the proposal to make sure that it is included.

Some consultancies tend to include the CVs of senior people who won't be working on the project, in an effort to impress the client. Most clients will recognize this ploy and it can easily backfire on you. You don't want to be asked, some way into the project, 'When is so-and-so going to become involved?'

By all means keep CVs on disk ready to drop into proposals, but don't forget to tailor them to fit the project in hand. Using a standard CV for every proposal is a waste of a sales opportunity.

Outside help
If you are planning to use consultants from outside your organization, say who they are and what they will do. Be clear that you will be taking responsibility for their work (if that is the

case). Don't try to 'fudge' the issue or imply that they are on your permanent staff – the client is likely to notice discrepancies now or later.

Remember that in some businesses 'freelance' might have unwanted implications, suggesting unreliability or lack of commitment. If your outside help is from someone with special skills, you might consider using terms like 'consultant' or 'external advisor' or 'expert advisor' to make their use sound more positive – but be wary of appearing pretentious.

Selling the company – the Credentials section

Every proposal should contain a section outlining the particular advantages of using your company. You understandably want to show the client how your credibility, experience and commitment make your company the best choice for the job. Clients often ask for this – in fact, some may specifically ask you to differentiate between yourselves and the competition.

Although the blanket heading *Credentials* has been used here, in an actual proposal it's often better to use something a little more reader-friendly, such as 'Why use Smith and Brown Associates?'

It's customary to put this section near the end of the proposal, as a sort of finale, but there are alternative positions. For example, in a 'beauty parade' type of proposal where there is no specific project to be described, *Credentials* would come immediately after *Terms of reference/Understanding the need* and before *Costs*.

Even in project proposals you may feel that it is more important for the reader to understand why they should use your company than to know exactly what is being proposed. In that case use your *Credentials* at the start.

The following guidelines will help to ensure that the *Credentials* section does justice to your company.

Use your SWOT and competitive advantage analyses to provide a framework

Rank your strengths in order of importance to the client with your key competitive advantages at the head of the list (see

Chapter 2). Use this to provide a framework of key points for the *Credentials* section.

Stress benefits, not features

Make sure that any facts you give about your organization are seen through the eyes of the client. The important question to them is not 'What can you do?' but 'What benefit will it bring to us?' See Chapter 7 for more about benefits versus features. Here are two examples:

Feature:

> We have the latest computerized project management technology.

Benefit:

> Because we have the latest computerized project management technology, we will be able to give you an accurate report on the status of your project at any time. We will also be able to provide an instant analysis of the impact of any changes to the proposed schedule.

Feature:

> We have completed several similar projects for recently privatized companies in the energy sector.

Benefit:

> Our experience on three similar projects in the energy sector means that we have a special insight into the problems facing recently privatized companies, and a comprehensive knowledge of the legislation involved. This will enable us to offer specialized advice to your managers across a wide range of issues.

Show you understand the client's culture

Knowledge of your client's business culture will help you to focus on those strengths which you know to be important to them. For example, you may feel that 'reliability' is the strength to stress for one customer, while 'creativity' is more important to another. A service publisher proposing to a well-known chain store wrote a very effective *'Why use ... '* section pointing out the parallel between the 'quality, customer service and value for money' the chain store offered its customers and the 'quality, customer service and value for money' the publisher was offering them.

Give specific examples of past projects

The more specific you are, the more likely the client is to be convinced that your firm has the relevant experience for the job.

Non-specific:

> We have extensive experience of providing environmental services to the mining industry.

Specific:

> In the last 5 years, we have completed four large projects for companies involved in open-cast mining. These included environmental impact assessments for proposed new sites in Venezuela and Nigeria (Godig Mining plc) and land reclamation schemes designed for Northern Coal in the UK and Shale Enterprises in Canada.

Avoid unsubstantiated hyperbole – back up promotional statements with hard facts

Phrases like 'We offer unrivalled reliability and commitment to customer service' or 'Our reputation in the industry is second to none' are likely to put a client on their guard, especially if they have just read similar claims in the proposals of three of your competitors. By all means mention the 'intangibles' such as commitment, service mentality, or integrity, but try to back up your claims with facts – 'Our reliability and commitment to customer service is reflected in the fact that half of our work is repeat business.' 'Our reputation in the industry is well known; *Advertising Review* recently described us as "a powerhouse of new ideas".'

Use the names of past clients to underline your credibility

If you can, quote the names of firms for whom you have completed similar projects. Depending on your business, you may feel it is good manners to ask permission to do this. Unless you see the large numbers of clients you have worked for as an important selling point, don't put long lists of past clients in the *Credentials* section – it breaks up the flow and takes up too much space. You could include it as an *Appendix*. If you can't mention a previous client's name for some reason, perhaps because your current prospect is jumpy about the competition, or because you have a confidentiality agreement, you can usually say something like 'a recently-formed hospital trust,' or 'a multinational electronics company'.

Use third-party endorsement where possible

You may be able to ask past clients to provide references, if they and your prospective client are not direct competitors. If you are citing a firm as a reference, you *must* ask their permission first. When citing a reference, give the name and job title of the relevant person as well as the name of the firm. Third-party endorsement can also be provided by quoting favourable mentions in the national, local or trade press.

Consider using mini-case histories

Concrete examples can be very effective in persuading the client that you can do the job, but keep them short – no more than three sentences.

> In a recent project for a firm of estate agents with 14 branches, we were initially called in to make modifications to the network of personal computers. However, we discovered that most of the problems with the network lay not in hardware or software faults, but in the fact that staff were not adequately trained to use the system. We developed and ran training sessions for all staff, and have been retained to train new staff as they join the company.

If you want to include case histories longer than this – and they can be very effective – they should probably be in the *Appendices* section.

If you expect to be invited to present your proposal in person, it might be a good idea to keep your case histories in reserve, to give you something new and different to introduce into the presentation (see Chapter 14).

Use Credentials templates, but select them carefully

If the answers to 'Why use Smith and Brown Associates?' are quite similar for each proposal, you will save yourself time by drawing up a set of key points from which you can make an appropriate selection. For each proposal you should choose carefully from the templates to fine-tune the text and perhaps to add new benefits specific to that client. At all costs avoid inserting the same 'Why use Smith and Brown Associates?' section into each proposal – you will be missing an important sales opportunity if you do.

How long should your Credentials be?

If your *Credentials* are just a small part of the proposal, rather than the main thrust of a 'beauty parade', there's a strong argument for letting your readers take in everything at one glance. One page will usually do the job. If you are using lists of past clients or mini-case histories, you could run on to two pages. Much more, and your clients are likely to lose interest.

Should you include a company brochure?

But, I hear you ask, aren't our *Credentials* fully covered in our company brochure, which we'll be sending alongside the proposal? In a 'beauty parade', where you are providing a very general picture, your company brochure can be an effective sales tool. In project proposals, however, think carefully about whether your brochure really does the job you want. There are three reasons why you should be cautious about relying on your company brochure as part of the proposal:

- *Your company brochure will be generic, not specific*   It will speak in generalities and cover all the services you offer. It will lack the close identification with one particular client and their line of business that you need to clinch a sale. It may even reveal that most of your business is done in areas that are rather different from those covered in the proposal. The client will not want to feel that they are something of a minority interest as far as you are concerned. Even if this is true, there is no point in rubbing their nose in it. 'We specialize in helping companies to grow' is unlikely to go down well if the client has asked for your help with managing a 'downsizing' programme.

In contrast, the *Credentials* section can select only those aspects of your experience and expertise that are relevant to the project in hand. By default, this also gives the impression that these are among your *main* areas of expertise, which will tend to give your client a safe, comfortable feeling.

- *The content of the proposal has a higher chance of being read than your company brochure* If your client already has a heap of proposals to read through, they may give no more than a cursory glance to your brochure, assuming that the real 'meat' will be in the proposal.
- *Your company brochure may not be circulated alongside the proposal* If your proposal is being circulated to many different people, there is a fair chance that any loose 'attachment' such as a brochure may get lost somewhere along the line and fail to reach all its targets. You can safeguard against this if you provide enough copies of the proposal for everyone and bind in, or otherwise firmly attach, a copy of your brochure inside each copy of the proposal.

Summary

Selling the people:

- Recent, relevant experience – the most convincing factor.

- Important post–school qualifications, e.g. degrees and diplomas.

- Special qualifications such as languages.

Selling the company:

- Use your SWOT and USP analyses to provide a framework.

- Don't expect your *Credentials* to be the same for each client.

- Stress benefits to the client, not features of your company.

- Use examples, mini–case histories and names of past clients to underline credibility.

- Substantiate promotional statements with hard facts.

- Use *Credentials* templates to save time, but select and tailor them carefully.

Action points

1   Study the CVs included in your last proposal. Did they start with relevant, recent experience and list only relevant, higher-level qualifications? If you think they could be improved, ask everyone on the project team for the next proposal to write their own CV, using the guidelines given here.

2   If you don't already have a set of *Credentials* templates, spend some time drawing one up and explaining to every-one how it can be used. Remember to include key points targeted at different types of client, which you can select as the need arises.

3   Similarly, if you don't have one already, draw up a list of past and current clients, categorized by type of industry, that you can use to support your claims of experience.

4   For your next proposal consider using mini-case histories to illustrate your experience. Could you also add these to your repertoire of templates? Remember that if you are going to name the clients concerned, you will need their permission.

5   Set up a cuttings database in which to store every mention of your company that appears in the local, national or trade press. Think about how you could include quotes from these cuttings in your *Credentials* section.

9   Selling with the *Summary*

The *Summary* is one of the most important parts of the proposal and therefore warrants a separate chapter. You will be able to write an effective *Summary* only after you have completed the first draft of the rest of the proposal, which is why this chapter comes quite late in the proceedings!

Most people will read the *Summary* first. In some cases the *Summary* will be the *only* part of the proposal they *will* read. Therefore it should be put together with the utmost care.

The proposal *Summary* is sometimes referred to as an 'executive summary', because it is the section most likely to be read by senior managers. In other words, it is the part of the proposal which is always read by decision makers. This kind of reader is not usually interested in technical detail – they expect their experts to look at the technical information in the proposal and advise them accordingly.

Essential components

The function of the *Summary* is to encapsulate the reasons for the client to buy. With this function in mind, the *Summary* should include the following basic items:

Your name, company address, the title of the proposal and for whom it was prepared   In other words, the same information as the title page. This is important – the *Summary* is often photocopied and circulated to a wider audience than the complete proposal. Readers must know who is proposing and for which project.

A brief statement of the terms of reference   It is useful to remind the client what you were asked to propose. Don't assume that this is obvious. Some readers may have forgotten, they may not be aware of changes to the brief, or they may not have been involved at the start of the project.

A summary of the need you set out to meet   The reader must understand the needs that your recommendations are intended to meet. If you have included needs that weren't mentioned in the original brief, you should briefly explain why.

How you will meet the need   A summary of your recommendations and project plan will usually form the bulk of the *Summary*, except in the 'beauty parade' type of proposal. Remember to emphasize what the solutions will do for the client, not how interesting or ingenious they are. In other words, stress the benefits, not the features (see Chapter 7).

Why the client should choose your company   Remember that the parts of the *Summary* which have the most impact are the beginning and the end. Why not 'go out with a bang' with a list of reasons why the client should choose you? In effect, this is a summary of your *Credentials* section (see Chapter 8). Make sure you include your key competitive advantages. Again, stress the benefits to the client throughout.

> Wexford Engineering will gain important benefits from using ABC Consultants to ensure that your new plant meets both current and future environmental standards. We can guarantee:
>
> - *swift and smooth completion of the initial environmental analysis* – as a result of our exclusive access to one of the most advanced computer models available

- *rigorous compliance with UK and EU legislation* – based on the comprehensive knowledge of our in-house team of five specialists in environmental analysis and management
- *practical, economically viable solutions to your problems* – our understanding of complex requirements of your business comes from twenty years of experience in environmental management in the mining and petrochemicals industries.

Note how each point states a benefit to the client, rather than just what ABC Consultants can do. Never leave it to the client to work out why a feature of your company is a benefit to them. You can't afford to hint – spell it out loud and clear. What seems obvious to you may not be obvious to a client who has read half a dozen proposals in one day and seen the same sort of features in each one.

Remember that supporting statements about why your company is particularly well qualified to carry out the project can also be attached to relevant points in the description of how you will meet the need. For example:

ABC Consultants will first complete an environmental impact analysis for the new Wexford plant, using an *exclusive computer model developed by our organization* in conjunction with the University of Learningborough. Our *in-house team* of environmental specialists will then put forward recommendations for modifications to the plant design in order to *comply with both current and planned regulations*.

Selling points are in italic.

Optional components

There are other components that you may wish to include in the *Summary* for certain kinds of proposal.

A statement of who will carry out the project   If relevant, include a line or two on who will be the principal personnel, with perhaps a selling statement about their experience.

A reminder of key points in the schedule   The *Summary* is not the place to go into detail, but it is a good place to stress that key steps will be completed by certain dates that are of concern to the client.

Summary of costs   It is impossible to give a yes-or-no answer to the question of whether costs should be included in the *Summary*. Be guided by what is usual in your line of business and your own common sense.

Among the usual reasons put forward for *not including* costs are:

- The client may dismiss the costs as excessive if the full reasoning behind them is not explained.
- The client may be less inclined to read the rest of the proposal if they become focused on costs at an early stage.
- Clients don't expect to be told the costs beforehand.

On the other hand, reasons for *including* costs in the *Summary* are:

- The *Summary* may be circulated independently from the proposal – if costs are not included, readers will be irritated.
- If the cost is reasonable, particularly if it's cheaper than the client expected, it can be a useful selling point.

If you decide to quote costs in the *Summary*, bear in mind that the best figure may not be the total asking price. Your competitors may have excluded certain items from their calculations, which means that they are quoting a lower total price than you. Quoting the total asking price out of context can therefore lead to unfair comparisons. You may prefer to quote for a core part of the project, or a daily rate, whatever you think will be the most favourable to you and the least likely to be misconstrued.

One way around the problem of summarizing costs is to prepare a separate one-page *Summary of costs* to appear at the beginning of the *Costs* section. This is useful for two reasons:

- it provides a concise summary of costs which can be read and referred to for decision-making purposes
- it can be attached to the *Summary* and circulated separately.

The most annoying kind of *Summary*

For me the most annoying kind of *Summary* is the one that summarizes the need, but then stops short of summarizing the actual contents of the proposal. How often have you seen a *Summary* that ends 'This proposal makes recommendations for how this need can be met'? That's not much good to the client. If the *Summary* is to work, it must state what your recommendations are, and what they will do for the client.

How long should the *Summary* be?

The length of the *Summary* should normally be in proportion to the length of the proposal. About 5–10 per cent of the proposal length (excluding appendices) is a good rule of thumb. Thus, a typical proposal of 20 pages or less should have a *Summary* of no more than one A4 page. A one-page *Summary* has great psychological advantages. Most people will be willing to cast their eye over the first page of any document, but fewer will be prepared to turn over to the second page and even fewer will make it to the third. If you make a key selling point on page three, how many people will see it?

In a one-page *Summary* all your key points can be seen at a glance. If your *Summary* is just over a page long, maybe you can 'tweak' it to make it fit on a single page. If you have slightly too much copy, and don't feel you can lose any, it may be possible to make it fit by slightly reducing the width of the margins, or taking the type-size down one point (though don't make it so small that the reader needs a magnifying glass).

Should you use subheadings in the *Summary*?

People often hesitate to put headings in the *Summary* of a traditional formal proposal, but there is no reason why you shouldn't do so. Headings can be very useful for guiding the reader through the summary and highlighting important points. They don't have to be excessively prominent or take up too much space. For more information on how to use 'selling' headings and subheadings, see Chapter 4.

Summary

- A *Summary* is necessary in all but the very shortest proposals.

- Length in proportion to the length of the proposal.

- **Essential components:**

    - your name, your company address, the title of the proposal and who it was prepared for
    - brief statement of the terms of reference/need
    - recommendations/project plan
    - credentials/'Why use ... ?'

- **Optional components:**

    - who will carry out the project?
    - timings
    - costs.

Action points

1 Check your five most recent proposals. Do they all have *Summaries*? If not, why not?

2 Consider the *Summaries* of current and past proposals:

   – Are they capable of standing on their own if they become separated from the rest of the proposal?
   – Have you stressed what you are actually going to do for the client and the benefits of using your company?
   – Do your USP and your key strengths come shining through?

10   The well-groomed proposal

This chapter is about the small points you should pay attention to when polishing up your proposal – like grammar, spelling and punctuation. It also discusses the need for consistency in such matters as abbreviations, capitalization and hyphenation. Finally, it considers proofreading for errors, and how you can ensure that your proposal is error-free.

But, I hear you ask, how much do these things matter? I believe that they are important, not because I am a fussy old-fashioned stickler for 'correctness', but because I think that every aspect of a proposal should be as professional as possible.

This book doesn't set out to be a grammar textbook and I don't pretend to be a grammar expert. But I do advise you very strongly to take some care over grammar, spelling and the correct use of words. These aren't the *most* important things in your proposal – good ideas will sell even if the proposal does contain a *few* grammatical errors and spelling mistakes.

However, a proposal full of errors will cast doubt on the abilities of your organization. Clients might reasonably argue that a company that fails to pay attention to detail in a proposal will also fail to pay attention to detail during the project. And there is always the chance that the reader of your proposal will be one of those obsessive people who just loves to pick holes and sneer at you for your split infinitives.

Many highly competent and professional business people have problems with some aspects of grammar and spelling. If you are one of them, I don't expect you to waste your valuable time on 'going back to school' in an attempt to achieve a miraculous improvement. That isn't realistic. But I do urge you to swallow your pride and get practical help with polishing your proposal.

If grammar and spelling aren't your strong points, ask someone who *is* a stickler for correctness to check the proposal systematically for errors. It needn't necessarily be someone who is involved with the project content. In many organizations, the secretaries are the people who know about grammar and spelling because they've been trained in these matters at college.

Don't leave everything to your computer – while the spellcheck is useful, it cannot spot typing errors that result in a real (but wrong) word. For example, it does not know that you should have typed 'from' where you have typed 'form'. Grammar-checking programs can be a useful learning tool, but they are too time-consuming for everyday use, and have not yet mastered all the complexities of the English language.

For those of you who have little or no help when checking the grammar in your proposals, here is a selection of the most common problems, gleaned from the questions I am most often asked during business and technical writing courses.

Compare with or compare to?

Use 'compare with' when you are noting the differences between things:

Correct:

We have compared the costs of on-site maintenance *with* those of return-to-base-maintenance.

Incorrect:

We have compared the costs of on-site maintenance *to* those of return-to-base-maintenance.

Use 'compare to' when you are likening one thing to another:

Shall I compare thee *to* a summer's day?

In fact, you'll hardly ever need to use 'compared to' in business writing, so it's safest to stick with 'compared with' if you are in any doubt.

One further tip – avoid using 'compared with' where you can use 'than':

Incorrect:

We predict higher sales in London compared with Manchester.

Correct:

We predict higher sales in London than in Manchester.

Different to or different from?

'Different from' is the modern way.
'Different to' is the old-fashioned form, which has more or less died out.
'Different than' is acceptable only in the USA.

Less or fewer?

People sometimes write 'less' when they should write 'fewer'. Use 'fewer' when referring to things that have been, or could be, counted. Use 'less' when you are referring to things that are not measured in numbers:

Incorrect:

Trained operators make *less* errors than beginners.

Correct:

Trained operators make *fewer* errors than beginners (because you can count the errors).

Correct:

There is *less* rain in summer than in winter.

No-one would think of using fewer here. But you could say:

There are *fewer* rainy days in summer than in winter (because you could count the days).

That or which?

'Which' is used in a commenting or parenthetical clause. If there are a pair of commas, or a pair of brackets, it's a fair bet that you should be using 'which':

The Thames, which flows through London, is England's largest river.

You could take out the clause starting with *'which'* and the sentence would still be true. The *'which flows through London'* is just giving you some extra non-essential information.
    Similarly, you would say:

The program, *which* was developed at Middlesborough University, enables you to estimate materials for all kinds of building projects.

'That' is used in a defining clause:

The Thames that flows through London is heavily polluted.

Notice, no commas, and the material after the *'that'* is essential if we are to make sense of the sentence.

Similarly:

The program that we use was developed by Middlesborough University.

Verbless sentences

Normally sentences must have a verb.

Incorrect:

A good proposal shows how you can satisfy client needs. Such as quality, reliability, and flexibility. (There is no verb in the second sentence.)

Correct:

A good proposal shows how you can satisfy client needs, such as quality, reliability, and flexibility.

Also correct:

A good proposal shows how you can satisfy client needs. These might include quality, reliability, and flexibility.

Very occasionally, verbless sentences may be used for dramatic effect. You may be able to spot one or two in this book. Like this one.

Mixed singular and plural

'The questionnaires was collected' is obviously wrong.

Other problems are more difficult to spot.

Incorrect:

Each of our consultants have a postgraduate degree.

Correct:

Each of our consultants has a postgraduate degree

(because you are referring to each consultant, not the consultants as a group).

But:

The consultants have postgraduate degrees

(because you are referring to all the consultants).

Punctuation

Whole books have been written on punctuation, but that need not concern us here. If you have trouble with punctuation, you're probably making things too complicated. If you write short, snappy sentences, as advised in Chapter 6, many punctuation problems will disappear. Remember these key points about punctuation:

- The purpose of punctuation is to make your meaning clear.
- People read between one full stop and the next.
- Each sentence (the bit that comes between the full stops) should consist of a single thought.
- Commas signify momentary pauses within a single thought. If in doubt about where to place them, try reading the sentence out loud.
- Commas are also used to mark parenthetical clauses (i.e. material which is not essential to the meaning of the sentence, and could just as easily be put in brackets).
- Semicolons signify greater pauses within the single thought of the sentence. If you use too many semicolons, your writing begins to look very old-fashioned and pompous. It is often much better to write two sentences.
- The main use of colons is to introduce lists, or to separate titles from subtitles.

- Exclamation marks should be avoided in proposals. About the only place they are acceptable in business writing is in a friendly, informal letter. If you want to emphasize something, write a short, active sentence. Consider using a one-sentence paragraph, or highlighting the key point with bold or larger type.

There are two punctuation problems that are so common they are worth discussing in more detail – misplaced commas and misplaced apostrophes.

Misplaced commas

Where commas are used instead of brackets, they must be used in pairs. Thus used, they mark a parenthetical phrase. If the material between the commas was taken out, the sentence would still make sense.

Incorrect:

> Hendersons, which specializes in company law is one of the largest firms of solicitors in the North-West.

Correct:

> Hendersons, which specializes in company law, is one of the largest firms of solicitors in the North-West.

Can you use a comma before 'and'?

Some of us were taught at school not to use a comma before 'and'. This is really too dictatorial. Sometimes it is useful to the reader. It helps avoid the sentence sounding too 'breathless', and may help to prevent misunderstandings.

Example:

> Our concern for quality is reflected in our BS5750 accreditation, and in our Quality Circle programme.

Example:

> We will be responsible for supplying, maintaining and installing the equipment, and for troubleshooting any problems that occur.

Where does the apostrophe go?

In informal writing, for example, a friendly letter, or this book, an apostrophe can replace a missing letter as in *'don't'* (short for *'do not'*) and *'here's'* (short for *here is*). However, I don't (or do not) recommend you to do this in proposals. It might annoy a minority of your readers who would consider it 'wrong' or 'slang'. It is safer to use *'do not'* or *'here is'*.

The main use for apostrophes in proposals will be in possessives and this is where many people have trouble remembering the rules. Here they are:

Put the apostrophe before the s when you are talking about something belonging to just one thing, or to a person.

> Correct: 'The company's records' (belonging to one company).
> Correct: 'Gerald's memo' (belonging to Gerald).

But put it after the s when you are talking about something belonging to more than one thing.

> Correct: 'The companies' records' (more than one company).

The exception is the apostrophe used with it. 'It's' is short for 'it is'. 'Its' for 'belonging to it' has no apostrophe.

> Correct: 'The reading was twice its usual value' (belonging to it).
> Correct: 'It's usually warm in summer' (i.e. the abbreviated form of it is).

There is no place for the apostrophe when you are simply using the s to denote a plural.

Incorrect:

Our consultant's will evaluate your needs.

Correct:

Our consultants will evaluate your needs.

Can you start a sentence with 'But' or 'And'?

Many of us were told at school that you should never start a sentence with 'But' or 'And'. In fact, experts will tell you that this *is* permissible, and can often add to the dramatic effect of what you write. If you search through this book, you'll find examples of sentences starting with 'But' or 'And', where I want to stress the contrast with the previous sentence, or emphasize an additional point.

I'm happy to commit such 'crimes' because I'm talking to you, the reader, in a relaxed friendly way, and I hope you'll appreciate the dramatic effect. *But* I would be more careful about starting a sentence with *'But'* or *'And'* in a formal proposal. *And* remember that your proposal might be read by someone who delights in ferreting out sentences beginning with *and* and holding them up as examples of sloppiness or a poor education.

What about split infinitives?

Using a split infinitive is nowadays technically permissible, but widely disliked. If you're still in the dark about what a split infinitive is, it means putting an adjective or adverb between 'to' and the infinitive form of the verb.

A classic example of a split infinitive comes from Star Trek:

To boldly go where no man has gone before.

Another example:

It is essential to fully evaluate all the word processors before making a decision.

The non-split version would be:

> It is essential to evaluate all the word processors fully before making a decision.

Note that, contrary to what some people imagine, the sentence below does not contain a split infinitive, because 'we' are doing the evaluating. The infinitive 'to evaluate' is not used and therefore there is nothing to split.

> We will fully evaluate all the word processors before making a decision.

Common errors of meaning

If you don't know what a word means, it is a bad idea to use it. Some words are so commonly misused, or confused with similar-sounding words, that we *think* we know what they mean, and misuse them unknowingly.

Here are some commonly confused pairs.

abrogate (repeal or cancel)	abdicate (decline to take responsibility)
alternately (every other)	alternatively (offering a choice)
appraise (form a judgement)	apprise (inform someone)
it behoves (it obliges)	it ill becomes (is unsatisfactory and inappropriate)
comprise (a whole comprises the parts)	compose (the parts compose the whole)
definitive (stands as a definition of something)	definite (precise)

disinterested (unbiased by personal interest)	uninterested (does not find the subject interesting)
infer (draw a conclusion)	imply (give a hint)
mitigate (make less serious)	militate (argue against)
oral (spoken word only)	verbal (spoken or written word)
practical (workable, effective)	practicable (feasible, i.e. capable of being done)
refute (prove falsity)	repudiate (claim falsity, deny)

Achieving consistency

There are some aspects of polishing your proposal that are not so much a matter of black-and-white correctness, as of internal consistency. For example, it is distracting for the reader if abbreviations are not defined, or different abbreviations are used for the same thing. Likewise, readers can become irritated if units (for example, of time, money or size) are not used consistently throughout the proposal.

The simplest way to ensure consistency in these matters is to devise a standard method for doing them which is laid down in a document, and which everyone in the company agrees to use. You may already have such a document, usually called a house style manual.

If you do not, it will be well worth compiling one. Don't worry, you won't have to do this from scratch. There is no reason why you should not crib your house style guide from someone else. Perhaps you had one in another company, or can acquire one from a friend. Internal style guides are unlikely to be copyrighted.

Alternatively, you could base your style guide on one of the many business writing books available (see 'Further Reading' for titles). One of the best and most up-to-date, which you can use as your company 'bible', is the *Economist Pocket Style Book*. This gives clear guidance on everything from the use of dashes to county names.

To get you started, here are a few standard rules which almost everyone follows.

Figures

Spell out numbers from one to nine inclusive. Use numerals for figures of 10 or more:

> The pilot system will be installed at three sites.
> We will book accommodation for up to 200 delegates.

However, use all figures in sets of numerals if some are 10 or over:

> There will be 27 workstations in the Cambridge office, 9 in the Glasgow office and 3 in the Cardiff office.

Avoid starting a sentence with numerals where possible. Turn the sentence round or spell out the number.

Avoid:

> 569 people responded to the offer.

Use:

> The offer produced 569 responses.

Or:

> Five hundred and sixty-nine people responded to the offer.

Do not use two different numbers next to each other, as this can confuse readers:

Not:

> In 1994 27 Personal Effectiveness seminars were organized by Terrific Training.

But:

> Terrific Training organized 27 Personal Effectiveness seminars in 1994.

Abbreviations

Some abbreviations, mainly Standard International units of measure, can be used without being spelt out the first time. For example, everyone knows what is meant by mg, hr, min and so on. Similarly, symbols such as £ or $ are universally understood. For any abbreviation or acronym that is not universally known, the standard rule is to spell it out in full the first time it is used and put the shortened form in brackets:

> We have applied for a grant from the European Commission (EC).

Some technical documents begin to read like a mass of abbreviations strung together, which can be off-putting, especially for the non-technical reader. To help make this kind of document more reader-friendly:

- use only those abbreviations that are strictly necessary
- provide an abbreviations list as a quick reference, as well as spelling out abbreviations the first time they are used.

Should you use full stops in abbreviations?

The modern style is to minimize unnecessary full stops – this makes it easier to keyboard documents (an important consideration if you are doing your own typing or want to be friendly to your secretary). Thus, while it is not 'wrong' to put O.P.E.C. for Organization of Petroleum Exporting Countries, the more modern form is OPEC.

Similarly, it is not necessary to put Ms. Smith or Dr. Jones – Ms Smith or Dr Jones is the modern form.

Dates

Minimalism also applies to dates – 1 June 1995 is preferable to 1st June 1995. It is becoming standard style in the UK to put the number first (i.e. 1 June not June 1).

Note that different countries have different conventions for dates given in numerals alone. For example, 22.10.95 for 22 October 1995 may become 10.22.95. Check how your client does it, and use their convention as a courtesy and to avoid confusion.

Capital letters

The modern trend is to restrict the use of capitals to:

- the first letter of the first word in a sentence
- proper names (e.g. people, countries, towns)
- names of months and days
- job titles
- titles of publications and statutes
- acronyms.

Watch out for the difference between proper names and generic descriptions:

Thus:

> The Plodworthy Pension Scheme will be administered by an independent consultancy.

But:

> Plodworthy has decided to set up a pension scheme for its employees.

In headings, the modern way is to use a capital letter only at the start, and for the categories mentioned above. Thus:

The need for stress counselling within Peabody Industries

A few companies still use capital letters for all except the 'joining' words in headings, but in my opinion this gives them a very old-fashioned look and it is harder to type and check. Therefore, unless your house style dictates it, avoid:

The Need for Stress Counselling within Peabody Industries

Capital letters and full stops in lists
The use of capital letters and full stops in lists is a matter of choice, but be consistent. Many people use this format:

If the items in a list are complete sentences, start each item with a capital letter and end with a full stop, for example:

> Just a few hours spent on learning a few practical, instantly applicable writing tips and techniques could help your business development team in three key ways:
>
> - The selling power of your proposals will be doubled.
> - Your professional image will be enhanced.
> - Internal cooperation and communication will be improved.

But in the next list the items are not full sentences. They start with a lower-case letter and the full stop comes at the end of the list:

> This workshop will enable delegates to write quickly, confidently, and convincingly, producing copy that is:
>
> - clear
> - concise
> - well-organized
> - persuasive
> - error-free.

Summary

- Correctness in grammar, punctuation and meaning enhances the professional image of your company.

- Consistency is easy to achieve if your organization has a house style for matters such as:

  - abbreviations

  - capitalization

  - headings

  - lists.

Action points

1   If you know you're weak on grammar, spelling, or punctuation, find out who are the experts in your company and ask them to check your proposals specifically for these features.

2   Do you have a house style guide? If not, try to adapt one from another company, or buy an appropriate book (e.g. *The Economist Pocket Style Guide*). Brief everyone involved in writing proposals on what the style guide is for, and make sure it is used.

11 Keeping up appearances

As with almost everything else in life, appearance counts for a great deal in a proposal. It may seem unfair or even downright immoral, but clients often attach much weight to the cover, internal layout, typefaces and illustrations used in the proposal. How often have you heard comments about your competitors' proposals, such as 'It was a scrappy little thing' or 'It looked as if it had been thrown together.'?

If you are spending a great deal of time and energy thinking about what is to go into the proposal and putting it down on paper, it makes sense to ensure that your efforts are not undermined by a poor appearance. Presenting a scruffy proposal is like turning up at a meeting ill-dressed and unkempt – it implies a lack of respect for the client and suggests that your approach to the project is likely to be slapdash and unprofessional.

This chapter will help you to ensure that the appearance of your proposal reflects the highest standards of professionalism at a realistic price. Let's call this the proposal format (we could just as easily call it proposal presentation, but 'format' avoids confusion with the presentation of the proposal in person, as described in Chapter 14).

Here's a guide to putting together proposals that do justice to the ideas, ability and integrity of your firm.

What format is appropriate?

Before deciding what sort of format will be appropriate for an individual proposal, or for your company's proposals as a whole, think about the kind of image you want to create. What is appropriate within your industry? How much time and effort do you want to invest? Do your proposals have to tie in with existing stationery and binding formats?

What standard of appearance does your client expect?

Not all clients will expect the same standard of appearance. At one end of the scale there is the public sector organization or large company that issues forms for you to complete, or specifies the layout of the proposal right down to line spacing, type size and page numbering. This 'no frills' specification is in fact a very fair system, because it removes the tendency for readers to rate a 'nice-looking' proposal more highly than a scruffy one. However, it is the exception rather than the rule. In most other situations you will have a free hand to decide how your proposal should look.

As with the tone of the proposal, it pays to see how your client does things themselves. Their own letters, reports, company brochure etc. will give you a clue as to the level of 'gloss' they expect.

It is tempting to think 'the smarter the better', but this is not necessarily true. Some clients might be put off by a very elaborate format. If their requirements are for a simple, budget-priced job, an over-elaborate proposal might suggest that you are prone to add unwanted frills to the project and fail to control costs. On the other hand, if you are charging a high price for a very high level of service in a sophisticated market, your clients will expect your proposal to reflect that.

What kind of image do you want to create?

The image you want to present of your own company will be the main factor in determining your proposal design. A proposal from a high-tech computer consultancy will naturally be expected to use the latest in desk-top publishing (DTP) and computer graphics. A proposal from an environmental management consultancy might be less high-tech in appearance, but would naturally use recycled paper. A proposal from a firm of solicitors would reflect a restrained, cautious and serious attitude. There are as many different images as there are companies.

Should you have a standard style?

It is worth spending some time discussing within your company how you want your proposals to look. Your house style can encompass aspects of presentation, such as page layout, typography and cover design, as well as consistency in abbreviation and punctuation, as described in Chapter 10. A consistent proposal format has three advantages for your company:

- If the client repeatedly receives proposals with a consistent appearance, they will begin to associate the cover with the company. This helps your proposal stay in the mind of the client – a worthwhile advantage in a highly competitive situation.
- A consistent proposal format conveys an impression of good organization and stability, which enhances your professional image.
- Standardization of format saves you having to make the same decisions over and over again and makes it much easier to delegate tasks to a secretary or DTP specialist. It is also more economic to have standard proposal stationery designed and printed, if everyone in the company is going to use it.

What facilities do you have?

When setting a standard format for all your proposals, or for an individual proposal, consider the facilities you already have, those you might be able to gain access to, and those you might want to acquire in the future. Do this early in the life of the proposal – it's frustrating to be unable to implement a good idea to improve the appearance of the proposal, simply through lack of time.

Throughout this chapter I have assumed that nearly all my readers will be producing their proposals using a word-processing (WP) program running on a personal computer (PC), attached to a printer, or a stand-alone WP machine with integral printer. If you are one of the few companies still producing proposals on an electric typewriter, much of the same advice still applies. However, I would advise you buy WP facilities as soon as you can afford them. It makes the production of all documents so much faster and easier.

At the other end of the spectrum, a few companies will have full-scale DTP departments with specialist staff. If so, make the most of them, but don't forget the simple basic principles covered in this chapter.

Principles of proposal format

The remainder of this chapter gives some ideas on how to produce professionally formatted proposals with the facilities you have.

When choosing a format you will have several objectives in mind:

- to make it easy for readers to find their way around the proposal
- to make the proposal easy and comfortable to read
- to highlight key marketing messages
- to create an appropriate image for your company.

In particular, note that easy reading is not just a matter of proposal organization and writing style. Many objective studies have shown that typography and layout can make a marked difference to ease of reading. You can make use of these principles to produce proposals that 'feel' comfortable for your readers – which will leave your readers feeling that the proposal makes good sense.

Page layout

Let's look at the principles of clear and attractive layout.

Page breaks

Decide whether to print your proposal on one or both sides of the paper. I suggest you stick to printing on one side, unless the proposal is so long that thickness is an important consideration. Why? Because:

- you are less likely to make a mistake in the printing or photocopying if you keep it simple
- the client will find photocopying easier with a one-sided document
- readers are so used to one-sided documents that they may miss the information on the second side, simply because they do not think to look there.

Each main section should start on a new page.

Margins

A wide margin usually looks more professional than a narrow one. One inch (2.5 cm) all round is a fairly standard allowance. However, you may want to leave a wider margin on the lefthand side to allow for binding, particularly if you are using a form of binder that doesn't open flat (see p. 178). Or you might decide to leave a wider margin on the right, to allow readers to make notes. Beware of using very wide margins for the sake of good looks in long proposals – they could increase the number of pages substantially, making the proposal dauntingly large.

Space between paragraphs

A typeset book like this does not usually leave a space between paragraphs – it just indents paragraphs at the start. However, the modern trend in word-processed business documents such as proposals is to leave a one-line space between paragraphs. If you do this you do not need to indent paragraphs at the beginning. Non-indented paragraphs are:

- easier to type (especially if the proposal is not being prepared by a professional typist)

- easier to check
- particularly appropriate if you have many one-sentence paragraphs.

Space between headings and text

There is no hard-and-fast rule on this. However, a good general principle is to restrict the use of a one-line space under the heading to the most important, e.g. main section, headings. You will soon see that if you leave a space under minor subheadings, the page begins to be broken up, and it becomes hard to see at a glance which section the heading is attached to. The problem is especially acute if the heading is in the same size and font as the body text, even if it is emboldened.

Space between lines

Occasionally you will be asked to use double or one-and-a-half line spacing. This is supposed to allow the reader to make notes between the lines. Where you have a choice, however, I think that even one-and-a-half line spacing tends to spread the text out too much for easy reading. Large spaces between the lines also make for large and unwieldy proposals. Most proposals are fine with single spacing.

One option that I think looks particularly attractive is to use slightly larger than average type (13 or 14 point). This type size is especially easy to read and it also solves the spacing problem. Single-line spacing with this type size allows plenty of room for readers to write comments between lines, and yet does not look excessively spread out.

One column or two?

Most proposals use text which runs across the full width of the page, within the margins. However, a sophisticated word-processing or DTP program will give you the option of using two or more side-by-side columns (like a newsletter). A two-column format can look very attractive and makes text easier to read if you are using small type.

However, the two-column format can cause more problems than it solves, for these reasons:

- It can look too much like a newsletter, which could be disconcerting for some of your more conventional clients.
- It gives you more things to check – that one column follows on from another, that there are no bad word-breaks at the end of a column and so on. You can probably do without the extra work.
- It raises awkward decisions over what to do with large diagrams or flow-charts.

It's up to you, If you use columns make sure you have the time and the expertise to do it to a professional standard.

Justified or unjustified?

Assuming you have a fairly sophisticated word processor, you will have to decide whether your body text will be fully justified or left-justified.

Left-justified text is flush to the lefthand margin but ragged on the right, like this paragraph. Left-justified text is quite normal for word-processed documents and has the advantage that it avoids 'rivers' (see below). However, some people feel that the ragged righthand margin looks untidy.

Fully-justified text is flush on both the lefthand and righthand margins. The word processor inserts gaps between the words and letters to ensure that the type fills the full width of the column. This looks very smart (because it is reminiscent of a printed book). However, if you have large blocks of text you sometimes find that distracting 'rivers' of white space snake their way down the page. This is not usually a problem with proposals and, on the whole, I prefer fully-justified text.

Fonts

You may be used to seeing only one font coming out of your printer, but you may have more options than you think. Your selection of fonts is determined by your WP program and what instructions your printer can accept. The most sophisticated WP and DTP programs, combined with a top-of-the-range printer, offer a bewildering array of fonts, and even the most basic program usually has a choice of three or four.

WP programs often run on a 'default setting' to produce a printout that looks very much like what you get from a typewriter (often called 'Courier'). Many word-processor users are unaware of the full range of fonts that can be produced by their program and printer. Investigate and you may find a font that looks more elegant and professional.

If you are not happy with your range of fonts, you might want to consider buying additional font software for your computer and/or font cartridges for your printer to increase your options. But make sure before you buy new software that it can be used with your existing set-up.

How do you choose between the fonts available to you? Let's look first at the body text, and then at the headlines.

Fonts in body text

Prefer serif to sans-serif fonts in body text   Most experts on typography agree that, for large blocks of continuous text, a serif font is more readable than a sans-serif font. In other words, a font like **Times** that has little 'tails' on the letters is preferable to one without, like **Univers**. If you look, you will see that the body text of most books and newspapers is printed in serif type, though sans-serif may be used for the headings.

Prefer proportional spacing   Type is easier to read if it has proportional spacing – that is, if the spaces between the letters are adjusted according to the shape of the letter. Proportional spacing is standard with many of the fonts such as Times, offered by WP programs. One of the reasons old- fashioned typewriter output is relatively difficult to read is that the spaces between the letters are all exactly the same whatever their shape.

In full-width body text, use 12–14 point type   Full-width text on an A4 page is easier to read if it is in 12-point type, or even a little larger – say 13 or 14-point. As described above, type a little larger than the standard 12-point automatically gives you spacing between the lines that looks in proportion and yet allows reviewers to write between the lines if they wish. One company I know produces all its proposals in 14-point Times and they look very smart, but it should be noted that none of their proposals is very long and they can therefore afford the extra bulk that a slightly larger-than-normal typeface entails.

If you use smaller than 12-point type, think about using columns You may be tempted to use a smaller than average type size in the hope of squeezing more on a page. However, if you try to read an A4 solid page of text in 10-point (the size used for many books), you will quickly become tired. This is partly because there are too many words to a line – more than 10 or 12 words per line begins to make the reader uncomfortable. Do not go smaller than 12-point unless you have a pressing reason. If you do use a small type size consider using two columns (see p. 170) in order to reduce the number of words per line.

Distinguish table and figure captions from body text   If you have figures or tables within your text, make sure that their captions do not become confused with the body text – they could easily look like a one-sentence paragraph. Figure and table captions may be distinguished from the body text by emboldening or italics, or by putting them within the figure or table box.

If you want to highlight large areas of text, use bold rather than italic To highlight a whole block of text, for example, a summary paragraph or a key benefit, use **bold** type. Large blocks of *italic* text are difficult to read and do not stand out from the page at first glance. In contrast, large blocks of bold type are easy to read and scream **'Read me, I am important!'** as soon as you look at the page. Beware, however, of peppering every page with vast quantities of bold type – the impact will be lost if everything seems to be important.

Fonts in headings

No more than three levels of heading   As discussed in Chapter 4, it's good to have different 'levels' of heading (usually different sizes), to distinguish between sections and subsections, and to indicate your hierarchy of ideas. But too many levels of heading are hard for the reader to follow, and their benefit is lost.

You will probably want very big headings for the main sections or chapters, somewhat smaller headings for the subsections within the chapter, and yet smaller headings for the sub-subsections. This smallest level of heading will probably be in the same size as the body text but emboldened or italicized.

If you need even smaller levels of subdivision you can highlight the first word or words of a paragraph using bold or italics, as in this section.

Use either serif or sans-serif fonts in headings, but not too many different fonts   Sans-serif type is easier to read when it is big, so there is no reason why you can't use it in headings. However, it's wise to avoid using more than two different fonts in the whole document – unless very skilfully handled, a wide range of different fonts can look irritatingly busy. Also, the more fonts you use, the more trouble the document will be to type and to check.

Use capitals only for the highest level of heading – or not at all   Research shows that, although they attract attention, capitals are harder to read than lower-case letters. That's why motorway signs are always lower-case. If you want readers to understand your headings first-time round, it's better to keep to lower case. You can use capitals if you want to in the largest grade of heading e.g. **UNDERSTANDING THE NEED**.

Italics in headings should also be emboldened   Italics are often used for subheadings, but they can look thin and weak compared to the body text beneath. If you use italics in a heading, make sure they are also emboldened and maybe in a larger type size. The best use for italics is to draw attention to *single words or phrases* in the body text, which readers are conditioned to seeing as a mark of emphasis.

Consider whether underlining gives the right image   Underlining can be a useful way of marking headings, but its popularity has dwindled since modern WP programs and printers have made it easy to embolden text and use variable sizes of type. The current trend is towards word-processed text that looks more and more like print, and underlining is therefore falling out of favour. Nevertheless, it can still be effective. Experiment to see whether underlining looks right for *your* proposal.

The importance of print quality

Output from laser or inkjet printers has a clean, sharp appearance that makes your proposal look smart and professional. Some dot-matrix printers are also good, but the more basic models (with fewer dots per inch) tend to produce output that is slightly fuzzy, and harder to read than laser or inkjet output.

If your dot-matrix printer is adequate for all your daily needs, but you would like to produce something smarter for proposals, you could look into whether a local WP bureau, or maybe another department in your organization, can take your floppy disks and use them with their computer and printer to produce smarter output for special occasions. But be wary – the downside of this arrangement will be that it is harder to make last-minute changes, or correct that typing error you always find just as you are about to drop the proposal in the post.

Tables and graphics

Again, your software and your printer will determine what kind of tables, graphs, charts and illustrations you can produce. For example, you may be able to produce tables in 'landscape' format (i.e. sideways to the normal 'portrait' direction). This can be useful for wide tables of costs or schedules.

You may already have, or be able to gain access to, software that will produce bar charts, pie charts, flow diagrams, Gantt charts, etc. In some proposals, graphics will play a vital part in making your meaning clear – a picture really can paint a thousand words.

Used appropriately, clear well-designed graphics can also add a professional 'gloss' and interest to your proposal. Never use graphics just as a gimmick, however, and avoid the 'creeping clipart syndrome'. Most people are now familiar with what computers can do and won't be particularly impressed by little pictures of computers or other 'business images' popping up in irrelevant places.

Paper

Standard white paper
There is nothing wrong with plain white good quality photo-copier paper – in fact, it will usually be your first choice. This basic office paper is always readily available, whereas a more unusual paper might run out just when you need it – usually outside the opening hours of your stationery supplier. Plain white paper also has the advantage that photocopies look and feel just like the original.

Coloured, textured and heavyweight papers
You might want to be more adventurous, especially if your organization is already using a special paper for its letterhead. A textured or extra-heavy white paper, for example, always creates a classy effect. You might also consider using coloured paper, either for the whole proposal or to distinguish particular sections. You could select the colour to reflect the tone of your organization – cream, blue, grey, green and buff are generally considered to be 'serious' colours. You need confidence to use pink, lemon yellow or lavender!

If you use plain white photocopier paper throughout a long proposal, consider inserting sheets of coloured paper to divide main sections (see Divider cards below).

Avoid strong tones of coloured paper for text pages, because they can 'compete' with the type and make it more difficult to read. Remember also that if your proposal is photocopied once it leaves your hands, the impact of the coloured or textured paper will be lost.

Logos

Your logo

In addition to their letterhead incorporating their logo, company name and address, many companies also have run-on paper with just the logo and maybe the company name. Thus, the reader is subtly reminded on every page of who produced the document – a great advantage in a proposal. If you do not have such paper, consider having some printed. If this is too expensive, you could use your company name as a 'running head' or 'running foot', i.e. printed at the top or the bottom of every page. Many WP programs will do this automatically. It's a good idea to insert a rule either right across the page or just under the running head to distinguish it clearly from the body text.

Naturally, your company name and logo should also appear prominently on the cover and title page of the proposal.

Your client's logo

Consider whether you want to use your client's logo in some way in your proposal – maybe on the cover. I used to work with a business development manager who argued that using the client's logo was akin to using the client's name and 'you' language in the proposal. He claimed it would give the client a nice warm feeling to see their logo in a prominent position. He was certainly very successful with his proposals, though there's no way of knowing whether it was because of the logos.

If you want to try this technique, you can duplicate your client's logo by photocopying. Or, if you have the facilities, you can scan it and incorporate it into your computer file as a bitmapped image (which can be resized and manipulated at will). Beware, however, of the sin of 'logo abuse'. Many companies have strict rules about how their logo can be used, how it should be positioned in relation to the company name, and so on. It does not create a good impression to borrow your client's logo and then use it in a way of which they would disapprove.

Colour

If you have a colour printer, you might consider using colour for your headings and in diagrams and illustrations. Studies show that most people are attracted by colour in printed material, but it seems to be more important to poorly educated and younger readers.

Assuming that most of your readers are likely to be well-educated, and many will be of mature years, the message seems to be that colour should only be used discreetly and appropriately. But colour is more than a gimmick – it can add to the information content. For example, a flow chart showing how different steps of a project tie together could use colour to distinguish the steps carried out by you, those carried out by the client, and those contracted out to other suppliers.

If you use colour remember that all your efforts may be in vain if the proposal is photocopied by the client. It is worth checking the results of this – for example, if you use black type in a coloured box and it is photocopied, will the type then disappear into a dark grey box?

Binding

Unless your brief specifies otherwise, I think proposals – even short ones – should always be bound within stiff covers (see below). A bound proposal looks and feels substantial and professional and also ensures that pages do not go missing. Many companies like to bind a copy of the covering letter in with the proposal, to ensure that every reader has the chance to see the key benefits the covering letter stresses.

The usual options are wire- or comb-binding and thermal binding. The advantage of wire- or comb-binding is that the proposal can be opened flat, which makes life easier for the reader. Thermal binding looks smart for thin documents but they cannot be opened flat. I prefer comb-binding to wire-binding as it gives a smooth spine which can be co-ordinated with your company colours.

Check whether there is a wire- or comb-binding or thermal binding machine somewhere in your company. If not, you might consider taking the proposal to a local copy shop or WP agency for binding, though again this makes last-minute binding a risky business.

Covers

It is worth spending time and effort on choosing the right cover for your proposal. A good first impression stays in the mind, and a bad one is similarly hard to eradicate. It's well known that in job interviews the interviewer's mind is usually made up in the first few minutes. Proposals have more of a chance to make their case, but a good first impression is still crucial.

Cover copy

As discussed in Chapter 3, your proposal will have a title page which gives all the important details such as what the proposal is for, who prepared it, who requested it, code numbers, and so on.

Assuming that all this is inside, your cover can be very simple. You may want to keep it to 'Proposal for whatever the project is … ' and your company name. Some proposal covers give nothing but the company name and logo of the proposer (i.e. standard covers that are used for all sorts of company documents). This may not be a good idea – you do want your proposal to be clearly identifiable when it is lying among a pile of other material on someone's desk.

Cover options

Let's assume that your proposal is being bound between stiff covers, rather than placed in a ring-binder. We shall exclude the proposals that have no cover because the client's rules specify otherwise. You have three basic options, all of which can be very effective:

- transparent plastic covers, revealing a title page or cover page beneath
- plain card covers, with or without a window
- printed card covers, with or without a window.

Transparent plastic covers are one of the cheaper options. They provide a protective barrier against marks and tears, while revealing the WP output on ordinary paper beneath. One option is simply to have the title page of your proposal visible through the transparent plastic cover.

You may want to be a little more creative than this. You could have a sheet of your company letterhead with the proposal title printed across the middle of the page in large type. Or you could design a special cover which could nevertheless be easily produced on plain white photocopier paper. One firm of consultants who provide environmental consultancy to the open-cast mining industry use a photocopied black-and-white image of an open-cast mining site, with the proposal title and their company name emblazoned across it – simple and cheap, but very effective.

Plain card covers are available in white or coloured card. If you consult a specialist supplier you will find a good selection of strong colours and also some textured cards (e.g. 'leather' effect). You may be able to find a colour which matches your company colours. You can put the card through your printer to create a printed cover, or use a card with a window and type the title and your company name in the right spot on the page beneath. You can use a larger type size if you print on the cover card and the proposal looks more personalized. If your printer will not take card, you can use a large stick-on label, but it needs to be very carefully done to avoid looking scruffy.

Printed card covers provide the most professional-looking option, if you can afford them. Think carefully about what to have printed on the card, and whether or not you want a window. Will the printing be on the front cover only, or do you want a printed back cover as well?

You may elect to have just 'Proposal' and your company name and logo on the front cover card. This is fine unless the client is likely to have more than one proposal from you at any one time. In this case it will be important to show the title on the front page, either by using a window or by overprinting directly on the card. You could use a stick-on label but, on this kind of smart cover, it looks very much like an afterthought.

The sky is the limit with a printed cover. It is worth consulting a professional graphic designer, who will be able to come up with a design that expresses the image you want to create, and also integrates with any existing stationery.

Talk to the designer about the many special effects available, e.g. varnishes for a 'glossy' effect, metallic inks, embossing, and so on. But spend your money wisely. A smart cover is no use if it means you have less time and money to spend on developing its contents.

Divider cards

If your proposal is very long, consider whether it would be helpful to the reader to divide it into sections using divider cards, or sheets of coloured paper.

Summary

- The right physical format can make an important contribution to the effectiveness of your proposal.

- When choosing your format, take into account ease of reading, the image you want to create, and the resources at your disposal.

- Use a serif font for body text, at least 12-point size.

- Allow a minimum one-inch (2.5 cm) margin all round – more may be needed for binding.

- Use a good quality paper, perhaps printed with your logo.

- Unless regulations say otherwise, bind your proposal within card covers.

- Consider having your cover specially designed and printed, or use coloured card from a stationery supplier.

Action points

1   Review the page layout and typography of your last few proposals:

   - Is there a consistent company style and are you satisfied with it?
   - Have you used a serif font for the body text? Is it big enough?
   - Have you used appropriate sizes and styles of fonts in the headings?
   - Are there too many gaps between the headings and the body text?
   - Are the margins wide enough?

2   Review the facilities you have for producing your proposals:

   - Is print quality from your printer good enough?
   - Do your word processor and printer offer an adequate range of fonts?
   - Do you have binding facilities in the office or at a local copy-shop?

3   Review the stationery you use for producing proposals:

   - Is it worth having your company logo printed on all your paper?
   - Do you already have suitable covers?
   - Could you adapt anything that is already available, e.g. report covers?
   - Is it worth having covers specially printed, or could you use coloured card from a stationer?

12 Checking your proposal

When, at last, your proposal is written, it should be checked and corrected before it is finally ready for binding.

I use the term 'checking' because it covers a wide range of operations, from ensuring that the content meets the needs of the reader, to looking for mistakes in spelling and punctuation. You will hear other terms used to describe different types of checking, especially 'editing' and 'proofreading'.

- *Editing* usually describes changes made to the first draft of a document. It might include major changes like adding or deleting a section, or minor changes like revising the structure of a sentence to enhance its quality. *Copy editing* is a term sometimes used to describe changes that do not affect content or structure, such as putting the document into 'house style'.
- *Proofreading* is often used nowadays to describe the search for minor mistakes such as spelling errors or misplaced apostrophes. Some people would argue that, strictly speaking, proofreading can only refer to checking a printer's proofs against a manuscript or a previous set of proofs. With computerization that kind of proofreading is becoming less commonplace, and proofreading is coming to mean 'checking for minor errors'.

Confused by terminology? I'm not surprised. So let's keep to 'checking', and look at what needs to be checked, and how.

Proposals are usually produced on word processors and you can assume that all the guidelines in this section refer to word-processed documents.

Checking a typical word-processed proposal can be broadly divided into two tasks, which will often be dealt with by different people:

- overview checking
- checking for detail.

Let's look first at overview checking.

Overview checking

Who does this depends on the size of the proposal team and the structure and internal rules of your company.

Ideally at least two people should perform an overview check on the proposal:

- the proposal writer (you will surely want to read it through carefully yourself before letting anyone else see it)
- another person who understands the project, particularly its marketing objectives.

Real life situations can vary from one extreme to another. If you are a one-person consultancy, there may be no-one on whom you can call for an overview. If you are working as part of a team, several team members may want to see it. If you are working for a large company, there may be rules and regulations about who has to see and sign off the proposal.

Review of proposals 'by committee' can get out of hand. You won't want to figure out how to incorporate six sets of contradictory comments. You will want people to comment on the right issues. How often have you submitted a document to a senior manager to find it full of remarks about whether you can start a sentence with 'but'? Why couldn't they comment on important topics like the benefits to the customer instead?

Here are some ideas for avoiding these problems:

- Wherever possible, limit the number of people who will review the whole proposal to one or two who really know what they are doing.
- People with a special interest in just one section should be asked to restrict their comments to that section.
- Give reviewers a checklist of what they should be looking for (see below p. 192).
- If several people are reviewing the proposal, arrange a meeting at which you agree changes, rather than trying to amalgamate comments which may actually be contradictory.
- Check the proposal once for minor errors before you submit it to your colleagues. You will have to re-check once changes have been made, but a once-over at this stage will help to minimize inappropriate 'nit-picking'.
- Attach a note to the proposal saying something like: 'This document has not yet been proofread. A careful check for minor errors will be made once the content and organization have been approved. At this stage, we would like you to review the content and organization of the document, in particular sections ... '.

Checking for detail

I believe that two – and only two – people are needed to check the detail of the proposal:

- the proposal writer (who usually takes final responsibility)
- Another person who has an excellent knowledge of grammar, spelling and 'house style'.

Checking for detail is quite different from overview checking. The second reader can be someone who has no particular knowledge of the project – in fact, lack of knowledge can be a distinct advantage. Lack of involvement with the 'story' frees the reader to search for errors without being sidetracked.

It's rarely cost-effective for more than two people to check the detail of the proposal. Often there are many minor decisions to be made, which will have no impact on the selling power of the proposal. Someone has to go ahead and make those minor decisions. There is no point in taking up valuable time arguing over whether you should put a hyphen here or start a new paragraph there.

When checking for detail both the proposal writer and the second checker can use some specific techniques to help increase the chances of finding mistakes. If you are a one-person business, and really have no-one available to help you check your proposal, these techniques will be especially important.

Ways to increase your chance of finding mistakes

- *Take a break between writing and reading*   Sleep on it or, better still, take a couple of days break. If you are desperate, an hour or two is better than nothing.
- *Take your time*   You will need to read more slowly than usual. Checking is a time-consuming business, but a skimped check is hardly worth doing.
- *Take regular breaks*   Checking for half an hour, then a ten-minute break, is a good rule.
- *Don't expect to be able to find everything at one pass*   Several will be necessary (see below).
- *Read line by line*   Try putting a ruler or piece of paper over the text to 'mask' the rest of the page.
- *Make the text look 'different' to reduce your familiarity with it*   For example:

  – if you have been writing 'on-screen,' print out the proposal before reading it
  – print out the proposal on coloured paper, or put a coloured sheet of acetate over it.
- *Use a checklist to increase your concentration.*

Making several different passes through the proposal
Hardly anyone is capable of the concentration needed to check every aspect of a document at once. Most people find it easiest

and most effective to make several passes through the proposal, looking for different things each time. Work out your own technique for this. Not every pass will be equally time consuming – for example, checking the contents list can be completed in a matter of minutes. One effective sequence is:

- *Pass 1 – completeness*   Are all parts present?
- *Pass 2 – layout*   Do page breaks fall in the right place? Do graphs slot in at the right spot? Are there any pages that only contain one line or a word or two of text?
- *Pass 3 – headings*   Are headings used in the right places? Are they the right font and point size?
- *Pass 4 – contents list*   Do headings and section numbers correspond with those in the contents list?
- *Pass 5 – section numbering*   If you have numbered your sections and paragraphs, are they still correct?
- *Pass 6 – sentence structure, grammar and spelling and 'typos'*   Do the sentences 'read right'? Is grammar and spelling correct? Are there typing errors such as missing words, repeated words, unwanted spaces, missing brackets, etc?
- *Pass 7 – numbers in text*   Check all numbers carefully. The second reader should watch out for numbers that seem implausible (e.g. a 1986 delivery date when the proposal is being written in 1995).
- *Pass 8 – names*   Clients hate the names of their company, its products or its employees to be misspelled. Double-check each against the spelling in their letters to you.
- *Pass 9 – tables*   If you have used tables, for example, of costs, are the columns and rows correctly labelled? Aligned on the decimal point? Do numbers add up correctly to the totals? Does the table have a title?
- *Pass 10 – graphs, charts and other illustrations*   Are axes labelled? Does the graph, chart or illustration have an informative caption? Is it inserted at the right point in the text? Is it referred to in the text?
- *Pass 11 – references*   If you have referred to other documents, books or specialist journals, have you given a complete reference? If references are numbered, do they correspond to the numbers in the text?

- *Pass 12 – cross-referencing*   Are cross-references between one section and another correct? Are appendices referred to at appropriate points in the main text?

Not every step will be needed for every proposal, of course. As a bare minimum, I would make three passes – one for detail of sentence structure, grammar, etc., one for layout, and one for headings and the contents list.

The following checklist will help you to check the detail of your proposal quickly and thoroughly.

Overview checklist

❑ *Content*
  ❑ Does the content meet the brief?
  ❑ Is every topic that should be covered included?
  ❑ Does the content meet the proposal objectives?
  ❑ Does it address the points raised by the SWOT analysis?
  ❑ Does it bring out the key competitive advantages of our company/our solution?
  ❑ Does it answer all the questions the reader would like to ask?
  ❑ Is any information irrelevant or unnecessary?

❑ *Organization*
  ❑ Does it follow any rules laid down by the client?
  ❑ Is it divided into appropriate sections?
  ❑ Is the content appropriate for each section?
  ❑ Is material within sections arranged in a logical order?
  ❑ Is there any material that might be better presented in appendices?

❑ *Overall impression*
  ❑ Will all readers understand it?
  ❑ Is the level of formality right for the readers?
  ❑ Is the document clear?
  ❑ Does it bring out the benefits of using our organization?

Detail checklist

❑ *Does your proposal comply with the brief/invitation to tender?*
   ❑ division into sections
   ❑ headings
   ❑ number of pages
   ❑ summaries
   ❑ units (e.g. man-hours or man-days)
   ❑ separation of financial from technical information

❑ *Is it complete?*
   ❑ title page if required
   ❑ author/your organization
   ❑ name of person who requested it/their organization
   ❑ distribution
   ❑ code number if required
   ❑ contents page – entries match headings
   ❑ summary
   ❑ all sections of main text
   ❑ references/acknowledgements/appendices
   ❑ tables/figures

❑ *Are pages numbered?*
   Standard format is lower-case roman for preliminary pages, arabic for main text (starting with the introduction)

❑ *Headings:*
   ❑ first-, second- and third-order headings clearly distinguished
   ❑ logical order
   ❑ consistently worded
   ❑ capitals used consistently
   ❑ no full stops at the end of headings
   ❑ consistent centring/alignment
   ❑ match those in the contents list

❑ *Spelling:*
  ❑ English or American?
  ❑ must read as well as computer spellcheck
  ❑ double-check names of people, companies, products

❑ *Grammar:*
  ❑ incomplete sentences
  ❑ wrong use of tenses
  ❑ unclear use of – this, it, these, those, they, who, which

❑ *Punctuation:*
  ❑ brackets and quotation marks in pairs
  ❑ commas, semicolons, etc., correctly used

❑ *Abbreviations:*
  ❑ only used when needed
  ❑ common ones need not be spelt out
  ❑ others spelt out on first mention in the main text

❑ *Numbers:*
  ❑ double-check for accuracy
  ❑ one to nine spelled out (except when making comparisons, e.g. 'only 3 of the 14 shops made a profit')

❑ *Layout and presentation:*
  ❑ title page clear and attractive
  ❑ readable size and style of typeface
  ❑ adequate spacing between lines
  ❑ each main section begins on a new page
  ❑ margins wide enough for binding

❑ *Lists:*
  ❑ consistent use of numbers/bullets
  ❑ consistent indentation

❑ *Tables and figures:*
  ❑ layout clear and not unnecessarily complicated
  ❑ all referred to in the text, in correct order

❑   show what the text says they show
❑   title explains what is in the table
❑   abbreviations explained
❑   totals in columns add up correctly

❑   *References:*
   ❑   all references cited in the text are in the reference list and vice versa
   ❑   numbered references refer to the right reference
   ❑   references contain all necessary elements (e.g. authors, title, publisher, date)
   ❑   cited in a standard style

❑   *Are cross-references to chapters, section numbers etc. correct?*

Summary

- Don't attempt to find all the small mistakes in your proposal yourself – always ask at least one other person to read it.

- Take a break between writing and checking.

- Read through your proposal several times, looking for different kinds of mistakes each time.

- Use checklists to make sure you have not omitted anything.

- Don't rely completely on your computer spellchecker – there are certain kinds of mistakes it cannot find.

Action points

1 If you do not already have them, draw up checklists for:
   – overview checking
   – detail checking
   You can use the checklists in this book as an example, adding and deleting items as necessary.

2 Work out a series of checking passes that suits you, and use it to check your next proposal.

13 The covering letter

Finally your proposal is ready. It's printed out, it's bound, and it looks great. What now? Let's examine briefly the process of submitting your proposal. Depending on the circumstances, you may decide to:

- post it to the client
- hand-deliver it
- give it to the client after a presentation.

In many cases you will have no option but to post it off into the great unknown. For example, many public sector tenders discourage personal contact at the proposal submission stage. The client may expect to receive a large number of tenders and will use the written proposals to select a shortlist who will be invited to present.

In other circumstances the client may already have invited you to present the proposal in person. In this case, they may or may not want to see the proposal before the presentation. You will have to be guided by their wishes. If you have the choice, opt for presenting in person first, for three reasons:

- Clients prefer to buy from someone they know – putting a personal face on the proposal is very effective.

- You may be able to introduce some of the project team – having the right person will often swing things your way.
- You will have a chance to answer questions, some of which might not be covered in the proposal.

If you are not invited to present, you could still consider whether it would be appropriate to go along and hand over the proposal during a brief informal chat. This may be easier if the client is an existing customer and you are visiting their office for other purposes. In that case it is only friendly to deliver your proposal in person and briefly talk them through it. This kind of informal chat can be particularly helpful if you have uncovered some needs that the client didn't know they had – a visit gives you a chance to do some necessary educational work.

Suppose, however, that you are submitting your proposal through the post. You will need a covering letter. Don't miss this opportunity to sell. The covering letter treads a fine line – you want to re-stress your key benefits, but you don't want to repeat the summary of your proposal.

How long should the covering letter be? It is best kept to one page, unless you have had to submit your proposal on the client's standard form. This may not have allowed you much room to state the benefits or describe the credentials of your company. In that case, I would try using a longer more detailed covering letter that is basically a sales letter (as described in Chapter 3).

An adaptable format

Here is a format for writing an effective covering letter, which can be adapted to differing levels of formality.

Start as usual with:

- your letterhead
- client's name and address
- copied to: line if appropriate
- reference number if used
- date.

Then follow this seven-point plan:

1 Heading.
2 Salutation (plus optional friendly comment in an informal proposal).
3 Enclosed is ... or here is ...
4 Summary of what is covered (just a couple of sentences).
5 Three or more benefits to the client of choosing your firm.
6 What happens next?
7 Close in a friendly way.

Finally:

- sign off
- add your name and job title
- optional p.s.

Let's look at some of these points in more detail.

Heading

Use a bold or underlined heading so that the reader can see instantly what the proposal is about. The heading should not be more than two lines. It should follow the tone of the proposal – formal or informal as the occasion demands. Informal headings can 'sell' the proposal, while formal headings should be more restrained. If the proposal is in response to an invitation to tender, repeat the title of the invitation to tender (if there is one) and its code number.

Formal heading:
**Mafeking Street children's playground:
Proposal for renovation**

'Selling' heading:
**Playa Dorada Sports Complex:
How sponsorship could benefit Sportex Equipment**

Salutation

An appropriate salutation can be anything from 'Dear Sir/Madam' to 'Dear Mary' as the occasion demands. Find out the name of the person who is going to receive the proposal. If you can't, you may be forced to use 'Dear Sir/Madam' for formal letters (such as those to government bodies). In informal proposals, if you can't find out the name of the person you could try something friendlier, like 'Dear Managing Director' or 'Dear Purchasing Officer'. If you know the person, decide whether it is to be 'Dear Mary' or 'Dear Ms Smith' based on what you would call the person face-to-face or over the phone, and how they sign themselves when they write to you. If you're not sure, play safe and use 'Ms Smith' rather than risk offence by appearing over familiar.

Avoid offending people by making gender assumptions. If you are not sure whether Leslie Smith is Mr or Ms, ring their company switchboard to find out. If all else fails, it's better to write to 'Dear Leslie Smith' rather than taking a guess at Mr Smith or Ms Smith.

Ms is fast becoming a standard form of address, but if in doubt look for clues in the way a woman signs her letters. If she calls herself Mrs Anna Brown or Miss Madeleine Pearson, it's correct to write to Mrs Brown or Miss Pearson, but if it is just Anna Brown or Madeleine Pearson, it's safest to keep to Ms.

Opening friendly remark

This is strictly optional, but might be appropriate if you have recently had a constructive meeting with the person, or seen them socially. Thus:

> 'Dear Jenny,
> Thank you for an interesting and informative visit to the Wellingborough plant last week – it was very useful in preparing our proposal. Enclosed are three copies … '

> 'Dear Bill,
> It was good to see you at the Awards dinner last week – congratulations to Megabux for pulling it off yet again! As promised, here is … '

Enclosed is ...

You should include a short statement of what you are enclosing. Describe the contents fully so that if anything goes missing at the client's end, the letter can help in the search. You might want to mention:

- the number of copies of the proposal
- whether the proposal is divided into separately-bound sections
- whether there are any other enclosures, such as a company brochure or a draft contract.

One of my personal bugbears is the old-fashioned 'enclosed please find'. You would never say that to anyone if you were handing over the envelope, would you? It's more modern, and quite acceptable, to say 'enclosed is ... ' or even 'here is ... '. You might also like to refer to any previous discussion or meeting, which will tactfully remind the client of who you are, and that they asked you to send the proposal:

> Following our very helpful discussions at the Institute of Directors last week, here is a proposal ...

Brief summary of what is covered

Provide a reminder to the recipient of what the proposal is all about. You might be able to include this in your 'enclosed is' sentence, for example:

> As we discussed last week, here is a proposal for the management of Megabux Marketing's annual sales conference at the Scunthorpe Regent Hotel.

Or you might want to expand on it a bit:

> As we discussed last week, here is a proposal for the management of Megabux Marketing's annual sales conference at the Scunthorpe Regent Hotel. As you requested, the proposal covers accommodation

and catering, audiovisual support, programme development and stage management. The proposal also describes some new ideas for motivating your telesales consultants, including a quiz game with valuable prizes, which we feel sure will generate much excitement and enthusiasm.

Notice that in this case the writer has drawn attention to new ideas which go outside the brief.

Key benefits to the client

I strongly advise you to put some benefits into your covering letter, even though you will undoubtedly be repeating them in the summary and again in the body of the proposal. If you are concerned about being repetitive you can always use different words. But if something is important, it's worth saying in several different places to maximize its chances of being read and remembered.

You could bullet-point the key benefits and highlight key words in bold type, thus:

The proposal demonstrates that Splash Conferences can meet Megabux's needs for:

- *Reliability.* As one of the largest specialized conference organizers in the UK, we have the experience to ensure that everything goes smoothly.

- *Value for money.* You benefit from our extensive network of suppliers and the discounted rates we can command.

- *Innovation.* We understand what makes sales representatives tick, and have the ideas to help you compete in the tough world of telephone sales.

Three key benefits are enough for most proposals – you don't want the covering letter to be too wordy. The exception is when you are putting forward a proposal in a format that doesn't allow you to bring out the benefits in the body of the proposal, for example, if you are filling in a detailed questionnaire. In this case your covering letter will be more of a sales letter, and you can take some extra space to bring out the benefits of your solution and your organization (see 'Comprehensive covering letters', below).

What happens next?

You may already have discussed with the client what happens next. Perhaps they have promised to contact you within a certain period of time, or to invite you in for a presentation if you make it on to their shortlist. In this case you can finish by simply reminding them of your understanding of what is to happen:

> I look forward to hearing your response to these ideas at the end of September, as we discussed.

If you have not been told when the decision is to be made, but you are on reasonably close terms with the client, set your own 'deadline':

> May I 'phone you during the week beginning 20 September to discuss this proposal?

Close in a friendly way

You could stop right there, but some people do not feel happy with such a brisk and businesslike ending. The usual way out of this is the familiar 'If there is any other information you require, please do not hesitate to contact me'. The sentiment is admirable, but is the expression of it right for your customer? If they are very formal themselves, you might think it right to keep with the slightly pompous 'please do not hesitate...'. But if you are on chatty first name terms, a friendly 'If you have any questions, or would like any more information, please call me' might be more appropriate. After all, you didn't think that they *would* hesitate, did you?

How about a more creative close? This can often help give a final gloss to the covering letter of an informal proposal. Depending on how pushy you feel you can be, and how close you think you are to a sale, you might add an expression of commitment and enthusiasm, such as:

> May I phone you during the week beginning 20 September to hear your response to this proposal? I look forward to discussing in detail how we can work together on what promises to be a very exciting and unusual project.

or:

> I believe we have met your brief in a creative yet cost-effective way, and am eager to hear your comments. May I phone you during the week beginning 20 September to hear your response to this proposal?

Or why not try a final benefit plug:

> May I 'phone you during the week beginning 20 September to discuss this proposal? Splash Conferences are looking forward to using our unique blend of experience and expertise to help ensure that this year's Megabux Sales Conference will give your sales staff the enthusiasm and commitment they need to succeed.

Pushy? Yes! Gung-ho salesmanship? Yes! But *some* clients will enjoy and appreciate your enthusiasm – it is up to you to decide which ones they are.

Sign off

How you sign off depends on how you started. The modern style is:

'Dear Sir	Yours faithfully'
'Dear Mr Smith	Yours sincerely'
'Dear Bill	Regards/best regards'

Optional p.s.

The p.s. is a trick you'll see used in practically every piece of direct mail. The rationale is that people tend to look at the beginning of letters to see what it's about and then at the end to see who sent it. Sometimes they might even go straight to the end.

Now, a proposal isn't quite like direct mail – usually someone asked you to send it, so you don't have to work quite as hard to get their attention. A proposal covering letter is also often relatively formal. So, you may not feel a p.s. is appropriate – some people think it might look to the reader as if you have written the letter in a tearing hurry and have not thought the contents through properly. It isn't usual for a formal letter to carry a p.s.

On the other hand, in an informal, friendly covering letter the proposal can be a useful way of drawing attention to a key date, or of offering an additional benefit which might otherwise be buried in the rest of the letter. The p.s. can be a carefully calculated afterthought (if that makes sense). Thus:

> p.s.   As it happens, I'll be in your area on the afternoon of Friday 15 May. If you'd like me to call in to talk through this proposal and answer any questions you may have, please give me a call.

Comprehensive covering letters

The covering letter is especially important if the main proposal or tender is written to a standard format that allows you little room to state key benefits or highlight how your proposal differs from those of your competitors. Tenders in the construction industry, for example, where you are required to fill out many pages of forms on specifications and costs, provide no opportunity to say why your company should get the job.

A similar situation occurs with many large companies or government bodies, who supply potential contractors with a list of questions to be answered. These questions may not include what, to you, are key inquiries such as 'Why should we choose *your* firm?' or 'Why does your proposal give the best value for money?'

The covering letter can be a useful way of making sure that the key points are made, where the client cannot help seeing them. In these circumstances, it could reasonably run to two pages. The plan for a comprehensive covering letter might include:

1 Heading.
2 Salutation (plus optional friendly comment in an informal proposal).
3 Enclosed is … or here is …
4 Summary of your interpretation of the need (one paragraph).
5 Up to *seven* benefits to the client of choosing your firm.
6 A line or two drawing attention to any key paragraphs, sections or questions in the main body of the tender.
7 What happens next?
8 Close in a friendly way.

Comprehensive covering letters – A case history

Tomlinson Electrical is a family-owned and run firm of electrical contractors. They specialize in wiring and electrical control systems for large buildings such as factories, offices, schools, hospitals and leisure centres. They have a lot going for them – a good reputation with their clients in the public and private sectors, a technical whizz of an MD who designs all the systems, and a loyal and well-trained staff. But they are in the typical position of most contractors in the building trade. Their tenders take the form of detailed specifications and costings drawn up to fit a standard format designed by the client, with little or no space to demonstrate the many advantages they feel they have over their competitors.

They do have a company brochure which they send out along-side their tenders, but they rightly recognize that the brochure cannot be all things to all clients. They need to emphasize the benefits they can bring to individual clients and individual projects. They look to their covering letter as a means of bringing home the benefits of using Tomlinson's rather than one of their many competitors.

Figure 13.1 shows their first attempt at a convincing covering letter, written to accompany a tender for the rewiring of a college.

For the attention of Mrs J Wall
Estates Department

Dear Mrs Wall,

Further to our conversation of 24 May, please find enclosed
our tender for the rewiring of Smithson College, together
with our company brochure.

Tomlinson Electrical Engineering has been established for
over 60 years and has gained a good reputation within the
construction industry for high quality design and
workmanship at competitive rates. The name of Tomlinson
Electrical appears on numerous Local Authority and Central
Government lists. We were one of the very few electrical
companies to achieve accreditation to BS5750 first time
round.

The company is particularly proud of its record for
training and is implementing the Government's Investors in
People programme. We have experience in the educational
sector and have worked in many schools and colleges.

We trust that this short summary of our company, together
with our brochure, will help you in deciding to use
Tomlinson's for the rewiring of Smithson College.

Looking forward to hearing from you and assuring you of our
best attention at all times,

Yours sincerely,

Carol Tomlinson
Director

Figure 13.1   Comprehensive covering letter – first attempt

There's some good stuff in it – the good reputation, the fact that they're well established, their experience in educational establishments. But there are also some things that Tomlinson's weren't quite happy with.

One problem is that the letter states facts about Tomlinson's, but doesn't make it immediately obvious what they mean in terms of benefits to the client. For example, the fact the firm has been established for 60 years could be a two-edged sword. It might mean that the firm is solid and well established, but it equally well might mean that it is old-fashioned and might not be able to cope with high-tech aspects of the job such as rewiring the college's computer suite.

Likewise, Tomlinson's say that they are committed to training, but don't bring home the value of this to the client. The client might even worry that they are likely to be saddled with a lot of half-trained apprentices who are doing their learning on the job.

The letter also has a slightly old-fashioned feel about it – they want to be formal, but they don't want to appear pompous. Note that the letter doesn't have a header, which could be confusing and annoying for the client if they have several different tenders in front of them.

After talking the problem over with their new non-executive director, who had a strong marketing background, Tomlinson's came to the conclusion that they needed to do three things:

- Think hard about what their clients wanted from an electrical contractor, which might be different for different clients.
- Find a way of converting features of Tomlinson's into benefits for their clients, using hard facts wherever possible to make the benefits more convincing.
- Draw up a list of benefit statements that could be easily slotted into any letter according to what Tomlinson's judged to be the client's priorities.

After much debate, they settled on a set of benefits templates for covering letters (see Figures 13.2 and 13.3).

Tomlinson Electrical Limited   July 1995

Benefits templates for covering letters

Sheet 1: General points suitable for all clients

To be selected according to what we judge to be the priorities of the client, and used in order of importance.

Value for money service Projects are personally supervised by the Directors to ensure complete customer satisfaction at every stage of the project's life, including post-installation support. Immediate attention is guaranteed for even the smallest problem or query.

Good working relationships on- and off-site Tomlinson's believe that good working relationships with our clients and with other contractors are the key to the smooth running of any project. Our staff follow a company code of conduct designed to ensure the highest standards of service.

Completion on target – or earlier Daily monitoring by the Contracts Director and Managing Director is used to maintain control and ensure that each phase of the project meets its deadlines.

The quality you expect from an industry leader Tomlinson's was one of the first electrical contractors to be accredited to BS5750. We have consistently obtained top ratings from the National Institute of Electrical Engineering Contractors, which sets industry standards. We are also members of the Electrical Contractors' Association, which guarantees completion.

The best in electrical engineering design The technical expertise and problem-solving ability of our Managing Director, Barry Tomlinson, ensures that each system is designed and built to meet the client's needs, offering a complete service from concept to installation.

The reliability that comes with a trained loyal workforce All our managers and employees participate in comprehensive training and development programmes. Our low staff turnover is reflected in the fact that many of our senior staff have been with the company throughout their careers. Tomlinson's

Figure 13.2   Benefits templates for covering letters

```
Tomlinson Electrical Limited              July 1995

Benefits templates for covering letters

Sheet 2: Specific points suitable only for certain types of
client


Extensive experience in healthcare installations
Tomlinson's has designed and installed electrical systems
in hospitals throughout the UK, including …

Extensive experience in computer installations  Tomlinson's
has designed and installed specialist wiring to computer
facilities  throughout the UK, including …

Extensive experience in leisure installations  Tomlinson's
has designed and installed electrical systems in leisure
facilities throughout the UK, including …

Extensive experience in school and college installations
Tomlinson's has designed and installed electrical systems
in educational institutions throughout the UK, including …
We also have two senior directors on university, college
and school governing boards.

Extensive experience in industrial installations
Tomlinson's has designed and installed electrical systems
in factories throughout the UK, including …

Commitment to development in the North-West  Tomlinson's
participates actively in Northchester Chamber of Commerce
and Industry and local educational and training
initiatives. We have received an award from Gartside
Borough Council for outstanding services to the community.
```

Figure 13.3   Benefits templates for covering letters to specific types of client

Tomlinson's next attempt at a letter for Smithson College is shown in Figure 13.4.

For the attention of Mrs J Wall
Estates Department

Tender for rewiring of Smithson College, ref AX/980

Dear Mrs Wall,

As agreed during our conversation of 24 May, I enclose our
tender for the rewiring of Smithson College. Also enclosed
is a copy of our company brochure, describing the full
range of design and installation services we offer.

We believe that Tomlinson Engineering can offer Smithson
College the service it needs – the best in modern
electrical engineering design, installation and
maintenance, combined with traditional values of quality
and attention to detail.

Value for money service Projects are personally supervised
by the Directors to ensure complete customer satisfaction
at every stage of the project's life, including post-
installation support. Immediate attention is guaranteed for
even the smallest problem or query.

The reliability that comes with a trained loyal workforce
All our managers and employees participate in comprehensive
training and development programmes. Our low staff turnover
is reflected in the fact that many of our senior staff have
been with the company throughout their careers. Tomlinson's
continuing commitment to training has recently led to our
participation in the Investors in People and Records of
Achievement schemes.

A track record you can trust Tomlinson Electrical
Engineering has been established for over 60 years. We work
for many major national and international building
contractors and are on the approved lists of numerous local
authorities, central government and the Northchester
Regional Health Authority.

Extensive experience in school and college installations
Tomlinson's has designed and installed electrical systems
in educational institutions throughout the UK, including …

If you have any queries about this tender, please call us.

Figure 13.4   Comprehensive covering letter – second attempt

Summary

- If you can, present your proposal in person.
- Keep your covering letter short, usually no more than one page.
- Use this seven-point plan for your covering letter:
  1 Heading.
  2 Salutation/optional friendly remark.
  3 Enclosed is … or here is …
  4 Summary of what is covered.
  5 Benefits of choosing your firm.
  6 What happens next?
  7 Friendly close.
- Use a longer, more comprehensive covering letter if it is your only opportunity to state the benefits.

Action points

1 Review the last three covering letters you wrote to accompany your proposals. Did you:
   - use any pompous or old-fashioned phrases that are out of tune with the modern business environment?
   - include a header to make sure the client could see at a glance what the proposal was about?
   - include at least three client benefits?

2 If your proposals typically consist of filling in a form or answering questions, consider developing your covering letters into sales letters. Would it be useful to have a list of benefits templates to be slotted into covering letters as required?

14 Presenting your proposal

The decision to select a supplier is made, in some cases, purely on the basis of the written proposal. In other cases the written proposal may be only part of the story. Often, the decision will also take into account a presentation by your company. There are two typical situations:

- You may be asked to make a presentation in the first instance, backed up by a written proposal. This is often the case with so-called 'beauty parades', when the client is selecting a long-term partner for as yet unspecified projects (e.g. if they are looking for a firm of accountants or solicitors). In this situation it is best to keep the client's copies of the written proposal out of sight until the presentation is over. You want them to be concentrating on what you have to say, not leafing through the proposal looking for the prices.
- You may be shortlisted to give a presentation on the basis of your written proposal. This is more often the case with proposals for specific projects. It is logical for the client to cast their net fairly wide in the first instance to see what suppliers can offer, and then to close in on a few promising proposals.

This chapter concentrates mainly on preparing a presentation to support a written proposal that has already been reviewed by the client, but much of what it says can also be applied to preparing for the 'beauty parade'. Note that this chapter is not about presentation skills as such – there are many books, videos and courses that will tell you all you need to know about such vital matters as voice control, eye contact and body language.

What this chapter does show you is how to plan your presentation, taking you right up to the moment when you step across the client's threshold. It tells you how to adapt and add to your written proposal so that you can be as convincing in person as you are on paper.

Fact finding

If you are asked to present your proposal in person, you will need to find out as much as possible about the circumstances of the presentation in order to plan appropriately. Here are some of the things you would ideally like to know. For answers to the more straightforward factual questions, you can simply ask the client. Some of the more subtle issues may require the use of judgement, tact and imagination.

What exactly are you being asked to do?
- What is the starting time?
- How long is the meeting expected to last?
- Should you assume that the time allotted includes time for questions as well as the presentation?
- Will you need to be available for any other meetings on the same day, or for lunch/dinner/other social get-togethers?

Who will be there?
- How many people in total (this may affect your choice of presentation techniques)?
- Which members of the audience are involved in making the final decision?

- Who are the actual buyers, and who are the influencers?
- Are certain people there to comment on certain things, e.g. finance, technical aspects?

Another question you may like to consider is: Can you rely on all the audience being there all the time? It is not unknown for some panel members to rush off to other meetings halfway through the presentation. Rude though this may be, you should be prepared for it, especially if it has happened to you before with the same group. It's a difficult question to ask in advance, but it may be something you can check out on the day, so that you can be sure to give enough attention to the concerns of the individual in question before they disappear.

What facilities will be available?
- size of room
- seating arrangements
- slide projector
- overhead projector
- screen/white wall to project on
- flip chart
- video equipment.

If you hear a note of doubt creeping into the client's voice when they answer 'yes' to any of these questions, it's best to be prepared – take your own equipment or simplify your presentation (e.g. use OHP instead of slides).

How close are you to being selected?
- How many other companies are being asked to present?
- Is there any indication that the decision has already been made and that this is just a formality?
- Who are your competitors?
- Is this the final hurdle or is there a further selection stage?
- When is the final decision likely to be made?

Knowing how many other companies are being asked to present may help you decide how much effort it is reasonable to put in when preparing the presentation. Likewise, if you know your competitors well, you may know something about their presentation style and strive to make yourselves different and memorable.

What are the client's objectives in asking for a presentation?

- Is the client expecting to see different solutions to their need from different suppliers?
- Is the client more interested in company credentials than specific ideas?
- Is the client mainly concerned to meet individual members of the project team and decide whether they would be happy working with them?

The client will often have all these objectives in mind when they ask you to present, but a little gentle 'digging' may give you a clue as to where the main emphasis of your presentation should lie.

Decide on the presentation team

Having found out what is expected of you, you will then need to decide who should be part of the presentation team, both as presenters and as back-room support. The key factors in deciding who takes part in the presentation will be the client's needs and expectations. Your decision will be based on factors such as:

- How many people should you take in total? Be wary of outnumbering the people on the client's side, especially if anyone on your team could be regarded as superfluous.
- Who has been the client's main contact so far?
- Which members of the project team will be working most closely with the client if the project goes ahead?
- Which members of the project team are the best presenters, or the most comfortable in sales situations?

- Is the presence of a senior figure such as your managing director helpful in demonstrating your commitment to the project? Or will it be considered mere window-dressing?
- Do you need technical experts to answer potentially difficult technical questions?

A good rule of thumb is that no more than two people should speak in a half-hour presentation, or three in one hour, otherwise there is a danger of the presentation appearing 'bitty'. If the client's subsequent memories are confused by there having been too many presenters, they are likely to feel a vague disquiet about the whole presentation, which will not work in your favour.

The lead presenter (sometimes the only presenter) should ideally be someone the client has met and feels comfortable with. The lead presenter should certainly know the content of the proposal inside out and be a confident and effective presenter.

In a group presentation everyone should have a defined role, and the client should be made aware of that role. 'This is John Smith, our total quality management expert. John's here to tell you how we would work with you to address quality issues, and to answer any questions you may have on this aspect of the presentation.' Remember that anyone who doesn't present, or who doesn't have a clearly defined role in answering questions will be seen as a passenger – and the client will wonder how many other passengers they will be paying for if the project goes ahead.

Be cautious about taking senior people who will not be directly involved in the project, simply to add weight. You do not want to give the client the impression that the project team are in need of hand-holding. Furthermore, the client will be alert to any hint that they may end up paying for a senior person just to hold a 'watching brief'. If you do include a senior person simply to bolster your image, far better to be up-front and say, 'I'm Tony Wilson, the Managing Director. I'm here simply to demonstrate how committed we are to this project, and how important to us XYZ's business really is.'

Plan your presentation

Decide what to include and what to exclude

The first point about planning your presentation is that it is not just a matter of going through your written proposal with a few slides and some time for questions, especially if your audience has already seen your written proposal. Your presentation should offer the client something different, new and interesting.

When you present your proposal in person, you face a different set of challenges from when you present the same information in writing. In writing it is nearly always wise to 'put your best strawberries at the top of the basket', for fear that many readers won't make it to the end of the document. In writing, it pays to tell the clients the key components of your solution, and the key benefits to the client at the beginning (in the Summary). On the same principle, all the less interesting material tends to be buried in the Appendices at the end.

However, when you present in person, you do not want to give away all your key points too early. You have a captive audience who cannot escape. So you want to maintain interest right to the end and finish with a bang to loud applause (actual or metaphorical).

Your written proposal may contain information that is not necessary to present at all. For example, you might not consider it necessary to go into detail about technical specifications or cost breakdowns. Your audience can simply be referred to the written proposal if they want to examine these details at their leisure.

Likewise your presentation may include information that is not in the written proposal. In some cases you may deliberately hold some information in reserve to add interest and variety. For example, if you have some good case studies, you could describe them only briefly in the proposal, or not at all, and go into detail about them in the presentation. The presentation may also give you the chance to include material that would have been impossible to include in the written proposal, for example, videos, models or samples.

The written proposal will probably have a main summary at the beginning and smaller section summaries throughout. You certainly won't bother with a big summary at the end. In the presentation, however, the good old-fashioned rule still stands: 'Tell them what you're going to tell them, tell them, then tell them what you've told them'.

A sample structure
Every presentation will be different and there is no 'right' way to do it. But here is a sample structure which will help you.

1   *Begin with introductions*   State briefly what your firm does, preferably adding a positive note (e.g. the largest, the fastest-growing ...), but do not go into detail about your credentials at this stage – that will come later. Make sure the client knows why each member of the team is present (and make sure you know who everyone on the client side is, and who the key decision makers are).
2   *Establish why you are there*   Not everyone will know. Say who asked you to propose and, very briefly, why.
3   *Say how the presentation will be structured*   'Tell them what you're going to tell them.' You can begin to sell as you do this, by:

- making a promise
- stimulating the client's curiosity.

Thus you might say:

We are going to present a simple five-point plan that will ensure you will reach BS5750 by December 1996.

or:

We are going to explain how we would work with you to develop an employee appraisal system that will help you maximize the productive potential of each and every employee in your company.

4   *Summarize the need*   The amount of detail will depend on the circumstances. If you were working to a very tight brief, all you will need to give is a brief point-by-point summary. If you had to do a great deal of research and analysis to determine the need, this is the point at which you explain how you approached the needs analysis, and the conclusions you reached.

The objective of this phase of the presentation is to bring all the members of the audience up to the same level of knowledge regarding the need. Remember that some members of your audience may not be familiar with the original brief, or with the investigations you may have performed as part of the needs analysis. They may have read your proposal, but have forgotten what it said.

Even if your needs analysis has been extensive, limit what you say to the minimum necessary to support the next part of your presentation – the solution. If you spend too long discussing how you came to your conclusions about the need, your audience will become impatient or bored waiting to hear about the real substance of the proposal – what *you* can do for them.

5   *Present your recommendations and highlight the benefits* Again, this part of the presentation can vary enormously in length, depending on the nature of your proposal. If you have submitted detailed plans for a public relations campaign, for example, it might take you some time to go through each component. On the other hand, if you are a management consultancy, you may only want to summarize briefly the techniques you will use to investigate a particular aspect of the client's organization. Whatever approach you take, remember these three key points:

• Relate each recommendation back to the need.
• Stress the benefits, not the features.
• Beware of excessive technical detail – if you see everyone in your audience except the technical expert glazing over, you're overdoing it.

It is in the presentation of your recommendations that you are most likely to make use of visual aids. These need not be confined to illustrations on slides or overheads. Videos, models and samples can also be used to bring your proposed solution to life in a way that your written proposal never could. You may be able to bring relevant examples of past projects into this section to help the client imagine what they will be getting. Finish by summarizing your recommendations so that the client can see at a glance what you are proposing.

6   *Very briefly, highlight key scheduling points*   The presentation is not the place to go into detail about schedules. The audience can be referred back to the written proposal for this. All that is usually necessary in the presentation is to present a simplified summary of what will happen when. If you are able to meet the client's deadlines, this is the time to say so, clearly and confidently. If their deadlines are not feasible, state what you can do in as positive a way as possible and state you are sure that deadlines can be worked out which will satisfy your client's needs.

7   *Discuss the philosophy behind the costs*   Again, the presentation is rarely the best time to discuss costs in detail. But it is worth telling the panel how you approached the costs given in the written proposal. In particular, think how your competitors might have presented their costs, and how you can demonstrate that you offer better value for money. If you think you are offering a Rolls Royce, while your competitors might be offering a Mini, then say so. Or if it is you that is offering the Mini, state that, in your opinion, this project does not have to be large and expensive in order to obtain the desired result. In other words, think what awkward questions might be raised, either during the presentation or, worse, after you leave the room, and try to pre-empt them. The same applies to scheduling.

8   *Say how the client will benefit from using your company*   This is a key part of any proposal presentation. In 'beauty parades' it is the main part of the presentation. In project proposals it will provide you with a rousing finale. As in the written pro-

posal, try to substantiate claims with hard facts and examples and concentrate on those features of your company that provide a benefit for the client. This is also the time to highlight the skills that individual members of the project team will contribute to the project.

9 *Sum up swiftly and ask for questions*   An appropriate finish for most presentations would be to reiterate (in your own words) that you believe your firm:

- understands the client's needs
- has the ideas, the experience, the resources and the personnel to meet those needs.

If the atmosphere of the meeting is appropriate, it does you no harm to end by stating your enthusiasm for, and commitment to, the project; that you hope you will be selected, and that you look forward to working with the client in the future. It never hurts to state the obvious (i.e. that you want the job). Never grovel or appear desperate, but don't fall into the trap of trying to appear so cool that the client thinks you couldn't care less.

10 *Prepare thoroughly for all possible questions*   especially the awkward ones. Thinking about saving some ideas and maybe some visuals for question time, either because you know a particular question is almost guaranteed to be asked, or so that you can initiate the discussion in the event that there is a ghastly silence and no one has any questions.

Six steps to a successful proposal presentation

- Prepare thoroughly.
- Make it different from the written proposal.
- Make it visual, with slides, overheads, or other visual aids.
- Give it a human face – the presentation gives the client a good idea of future working relationships.
- Vary the pace, but keep it moving.
- Begin and end with a bang.

What kind of visual aids should you use?

Your choice of visual aids will be determined by:

- the information you present
- the facilities you have for preparing visual aids
- the facilities you/the client have for presenting them
- what is right for the size of audience and the formality of the situation.

Some of the advantages and disadvantages of different methods are summarized in Figure 14.1 You may decide to use more than one form of visual aid during the same presentation. Whichever method you choose, remember that the technology should meet the needs of the presentation, not the other way around.

Mechanical failures, such as having your slides in the carousel back to front, or the projector breaking down, are embarrassing. Much worse, however, is the break such problems cause in your presentation and their effects on your composure. Keep your presentation techniques simple and you will have more time and energy to spend on the proposal and on the presentation itself.

In my opinion, the overhead projector usually offers the most convenient, flexible and professional option for presenting proposals to small and medium-sized audiences (up to about 15 people). OHP transparencies are easier to prepare than slides and there is much less potential for horribly embarrassing technology failures. They are also easy to re-order if the presentation takes an unexpected turn, allowing you to remain responsive to the needs of your audience.

There are some situations, however, in which I would recommend 35 mm slides: if you are talking to a very large group, if you want to show many photographs – or if your company specializes in slide production!

Computer-generated 'slideshows' can also be very effective. They can be presented on a monitor to a small group or via an OHP tablet or specialist projection system onto a large screen. However, many companies will not have the technology either to create or present them.

Visual aid	Advantages	Disadvantages
Desktop presentation portfolio with flip-over plastic pockets	Easy to prepare using standard office equipment; inexpensive; can be changed right up to the last minute; can include photographs, pages from brochures, etc.; friendly for one-to-one presentations; no problems with technology failure	Suitable only when you are presenting to one or two people
Flip chart	Easy to prepare; inexpensive; can generate new material, even as you speak; no problems with technology failure	Can easily look scruffy; may be considered 'unprofessional' if your competition use other methods
Overhead projector	Easy to prepare with standard office equipment; transparencies are inexpensive (and you will often be able to borrow the client's projector); if carefully prepared, can look very smart; can move forwards and backwards or change the sequence easily; projector rarely goes wrong (but make sure you know where the spare bulb is and how to change it)	Can look scruffy if badly done (avoid handwritten transparencies); may be considered less professional than 35 mm slides; not so good as 35 mm slides for photos
35mm slides	Look very smart and professional; relatively easy to prepare with graphics packages such as Harvard Graphics or Freelance Graphics; easy to introduce colour; best medium for presenting photographs; good for very large groups	Can be expensive if you have to go outside your company for help; if the projector goes wrong, you may be stuck – and very embarrassed; easy to put slides in the wrong order or back to front; not easy to skip forwards or to recap; you will have to darken the room, which puts people to sleep and takes their attention away from the presenter
Computer-generated presentation (on monitor or large screen)	Can move seamlessly between media, e.g. still pictures, moving graphics, video; gives a very professional, high-tech image; possible to jump backwards and forwards with some programs	Requires much work to produce to a professional standard; may need to be produced by a specialist agency; PC monitor presentations only suitable for small groups; embarrassing if the technology goes wrong

Figure 14.1   Choice of visual aids

224

The commonest mistake with presentation visuals

The commonest error made with any kind of presentation visual is to try to squeeze too much into the available space. OHP transparencies are particularly prone to this problem, because it is so tempting and so easy to simply copy large chunks of your proposal straight on to the transparency. How often have you seen an increasingly bored audience trying to read vanishingly small type off a bright screen, while the presenter proceeds to tell them exactly the same words as are on the screen? Remember:

- The best use for visual aids is to show things that cannot be put into words.
- Not everything you say has to be accompanied by a visual aid.
- You don't have to read out the visual aid for the audience to take in the content.

The secret of professional-looking OHP transparencies

There is a sure-fire way of preparing OHP transparencies (or pages on a presentation folder or flip chart) that will convey the same professional image as 35 mm slides. *Treat them as if they were 35 mm slides, and apply the same rules to their design.* People are so used to the 35 mm slide as the 'professional' mode of presentation, for example, at conferences, that anything that looks like a 35 mm slide tends to share the same status. It's rather like the days when your child's school photo came in a cardboard mount shaped like a TV screen. Whatever the fashionable medium, other media can share a little in the image.

OHP transparencies look most professional if you:

- use a landscape format (but make sure it will fit on the projector)
- use a frame, either a cardboard mount or a printed border
- avoid hand-written text

- keep text to a minimum (see below)
- use professional-quality graphics
- use your company logo
- use colour.

How can you achieve all this at a reasonable cost and with the minimum of equipment?

The frame   Putting something in a frame always seems to make it look smarter and adds to its impact. Cardboard mounts for OHP transparencies are inexpensive and have the great advantage that you can write little notes to yourself on the frame, which no-one but you will see. Cardboard frames also stop surplus light from escaping round the edges of your transparency while they are on the OHP.

As an alternative to a cardboard frame, you could consider using a border created with your WP or DTP program, perhaps incorporating your company logo (see below). Or you could try transparencies that come with a coloured border already printed. Don't draw the frame yourself with a ruler and a felt-tip pen – the OHP will magnify every wobble.

The text   There are two basic ways of transferring text from your PC onto an overhead transparency – by printer or by photocopier. Your printer may be able to print directly onto transparencies, but remember that you *must* use special transparencies for laser printers or they will melt and could ruin your printer. You can also print out onto paper and then put it through your photocopier. Again, make sure that the transparency you use is marked suitable for photocopiers, as some aren't. You may well end up using a mixture of both techniques.

Avoid any handwritten or hand-drawn material if at all possible – as you would avoid anything handwritten in a letter or proposal, except for signatures.

Graphics   Charts, graphs, flow diagrams, line drawings and photographs can bring your presentation vividly to life. Use as many as you can. Graphics created with, or scanned into, your

DTP or WP program can be printed straight onto the transparency. Graphics from other sources (e.g. a diagram from a manual) can also simply be photocopied onto the transparency.

If your proposal doesn't lend itself to graphics, you can still add interest with logos, borders and colour (see below).

Company logo   Using your logo on your OHP transparencies always creates a professional impression, and helps to imprint your corporate identity on the mind of the customer. You can add your logo to OHP transparencies by using a printer or photocopier, in colour or in black and white.

Colour   Colour adds impact to presentations – use it if you possibly can. Here are some ways of adding colour to a presentation, starting with the cheapest and working up to more glamorous and expensive methods:

- Coloured OHP acetates provide a simple way of adding interest – you simply photocopy your black and white text onto them. You could use different colours for different sections of the proposal.
- Clear OHP acetates with a coloured border enable you to add a border and colour at the same time. Again, different colours could denote different sections.
- Coloured pens and highlighters can be used to add colour to charts and graphs, but have to be applied very carefully to avoid the 'home-made' look.
- Colour photocopying – coloured diagrams and even colour photographs can be copied onto OHP film, though the colours will not be quite the same as the original.
- Colour printing, with a colour inkjet or colour laser printer provides the most professional effects. Coloured diagrams and coloured text can be created using a graphics package. When printed out, OHP transparencies created this way look very like slides. Colour inkjet printers are coming down in price all the time. Colour laser printers are still very expensive, but you may be able to find a local DTP bureau or printer who has one and who will take your disks.

How to design OHP transparencies and slides for maximum impact

Strict self-discipline in the amount of text you put onto your OHP transparencies or slides will pay dividends in terms of the impact and understandability of your presentation. Here are some useful 'rules of thumb'.

In general

- Don't overdo the number of transparencies/slides – no more than one per minute.
- Keep to landscape format – it looks tidier and you are less likely to put it on the OHP/in the carousel the wrong way round.
- Keep it simple – if necessary replace one complex visual with several simple ones.
- Try to have only one key message per transparency/slide.
- For slides, light text or graphics on a dark background are easiest to read. The same is true for OHP transparencies, if you are having them printed in full colour.
- Don't overwhelm your audience with colour just because your graphics program allows you to. A maximum of 4 colours on a slide will look colourful but not frenetic.
- Give each transparency/slide a one-line title – this will add impact and help you identify them quickly and easily.

Text transparencies/slides

- Use bullet points or numbers to add impact to lists.
- Use lower-case letters for most of the text – capitals are more difficult to read and should be reserved for headings, if you use them at all.
- Use a sans-serif typeface – it looks clear and modern and is easy to read when projected.
- Edit the text ruthlessly into note form – no need for whole sentences:
  – no more than 7 lines altogether
  – no more than 7 words per line.
- Use transparencies/slides to outline the structure of your presentation and to sum up at the ends of sections and at the end of the whole presentation.

- You can progressively add points to the same list to build towards a conclusion.
- Remember that text transparencies/slides are no excuse for putting the text of your proposal on screen.

Tables

- As with text, keep it simple and edit ruthlessly:
  - no more than 4 columns
  - no more than 7 rows
  - round numbers up or down and eliminate decimal points where possible.
- Highlight key columns or rows in the table with colour.
- Remember you can create interesting-looking tables just with text. How about a table of the client's needs versus your solutions?

Charts and graphs

- Yet again, keep it simple and uncluttered:
  - no more than 3 curves on a line graph
  - no more than 7 wedges per pie chart
  - no more than 7 bars on a bar chart.
- Keep labelling simple and abbreviate where necessary to stop the chart looking cluttered. If you must have long labels on each column of a bar chart, set the bars horizontally – that way you'll have more room for the labels.

Case study

A firm of management consultants was proposing for a project concerned with the impact of new technology on the secretaries in a large company of accountants. The consultants had recently purchased some new presentations software and wanted to make full use of it. Figure 14.2 shows one of the first overhead transparencies they produced.

It contains some common errors: too much text; muddled organization; repetitive wording; too many different kinds of bullets; meaningless indistinct graphics and inconsistent use of capitals.

CURRENT STATE ASSESSMENT

◆ ⇧ Team agree key processes and questions

      ⊃ What time taken etc.

◆ ⇧ Team agree allocation of project tasks and timescales

◆ ⇧ Analysis of Process in Detail

◆ ⇧ How can New Business Process streamline each work task? and can some be obviated that are not adding value?

◆ ⇧ How long will new process take?

◆ ⇧ What will be percentage reduction in workflow?

◆ ⇧ Analyse how much time each secretary/admin. spends on tasks

Figure 14.2   OHP transparency – first attempt

ASSESSING THE IMPACT OF NEW TECHNOLOGY

- ◆ Consultancy/client agree key processes for assessment

- ◆ Detailed process analysis:

  tasks
  time

- ◆ Evaluation of effect of new technology on:

  tasks
  time

Figure 14.3 OHP transparency – second attempt

Now look at their 'cleaned up' second attempt (Figure 14.3). It doesn't provide such a showcase for the presentations software, but it's a lot more meaningful to the customer.

Now, Figure 14.4 shows a transparency in which appropriate use of graphics *was* made to create a simple, clean visual.

Provide copies for your clients

The client may appreciate photocopies of your acetates or hard copy of your 35 mm slides, especially if you cover material in your presentation that is not in your proposal. If you are not giving your client the proposal until after the presentation, you can bind in photocopies of your transparencies as an Appendix.

Rehearsing your presentation

Rehearse your presentation thoroughly, especially if you are presenting as a team. If you are in any doubt about whether you will be able to remember your 'script', make some discreet cue cards to which you can refer when necessary. *Never* read from your proposal, as you will lose all eye contact and rapport with your audience, and quickly put them to sleep.

Make sure everyone in the team knows when they will speak, and try to predict what questions will be asked and who will be expected to field them. Prepare yourselves for 'stage fright' by rehearsing in front of sympathetic spectators from your own organization.

Preparation can even extend to planning what to wear. You should be like your proposal – stylish, creative, memorable – but *safe*. If in doubt, aim to be just a little more formal and conservative than your client, as this shows respect. Not *too* conservative – remember that you also want to be memorable. I met a senior actuary (not a profession renowned for wacky style) who insisted that his pitches to pension fund managers were most successful when he wore a particular tie. This tie was just loud enough to be memorable among all the discreet motifs worn by his competitors. For women, image consultants recommend a bright red jacket for creating an image of enthusiasm and confidence.

TOOLS & TECHNIQUES

Questionnaires

Interviews

Process modelling tools

Report & data manipulation tools

Figure 14.4 Good example of graphics

A last word about rehearsal – don't leave it until the last minute. A bad rehearsal the night before an important presentation will only serve to increase your nervousness. Try to rehearse early, while there is still time to put right any problems that the rehearsal reveals. If you are properly prepared, you will sail through the presentation and do justice to your proposal.

Summary

- Find out as much as possible about the circumstances of your presentation in advance.

- Think carefully about the presentation team – no passengers.

- Prepare thoroughly, and strive to make the presentation different from the proposal document.

- 'Tell 'em what you're going to tell 'em, tell 'em, then tell 'em what you just told 'em.'

- OHP transparencies are often the easiest, safest, cheapest presentation medium.

- But 35 mm slides give the most professional image, so if you use OHP transparencies, make them look as much as possible like 35 mm slides.

- Rehearse thoroughly – but in time to make changes if necessary.

Action points

1   Review the transparencies or slides used in your last proposal. Do they have too much information on them? How
could they have been improved?

2   Investigate what presentation software is already available
within your company. Most software can be used to prepare
either overhead transparencies, 35 mm slides, or a computer
slideshow. Could you use presentation software to improve
your proposal presentations?

15 Learning from experience

So, you've submitted your proposal and made your presentation. What next? It may often take the client weeks – occasionally months – to make up their minds. You can do little to accelerate the decision-making process, but if you have not heard by the expected date you may reasonably telephone to ask if there is a delay, and perhaps offer to provide additional information. If the answer is simply that the decision has not yet been made, you will have to be patient. There is nothing you can do at this stage to influence the decision in your favour, and harassing the client for news is unlikely to win you any friends.

Eventually you will know whether you have been successful. If you have won the job you will be elated. If you have failed, you will be despondent. But whatever the outcome, do seize the chance to learn from it. A little detective work on which aspects of the proposal or presentation contributed to your success or downfall could make a difference to the success of future proposals.

Ask the client

If you have been successful, the client will usually be only too glad to tell you which aspects of the proposal won their confidence. This information will not only be useful for future proposals, it will also help you to understand your client's priorities as you begin to work together on the project.

If you have been unsuccessful, it can be a little more difficult to find out what went wrong. A minority of clients will have a definite policy of not discussing unsuccessful proposals. Most will be willing in principle, but apathetic in practice. After all, they have many other calls on their time. You stand the best chance of a helpful response when your proposal was a 'near miss', and the client is genuinely interested in working with you in the future.

There are several ways in which you can find out why you didn't win the contract:

- *By telephone*   If you have a reasonably friendly, informal relationship with the client, they will not be offended if you bring up the subject in a phone call, or next time you see them. You can simply ring and tell them that you're naturally a little disappointed you didn't win the business this time, but that you're keen to work with them when another opportunity arises. So would they mind telling you about their reactions to your proposal, and how it compared to the winning pitch?

  Keep the questions open to start with, so that they do not feel uncomfortable or pressurized. If they seem relaxed about discussing the reasons for your lack of success, you can probe a little deeper. Bear in mind, however, that the client may shy away from talking to you about sensitive issues – for example, if they took a personal dislike to one of your team.

- *By letter/questionnaire*   If your relationship with the client is more formal, you may prefer to write a letter expressing the same kind of sentiments. The client may reply in detail, they may reply superficially, or they may not reply at all, but at least you will have tried. You can increase your chances of a constructive response by asking specific questions. For example, were their concerns about the proposal in the areas of:

  – the specific recommendations made?
  – the experience and expertise of your company or personnel?
  – price?

Some companies that produce a very large number of proposals send a follow-up questionnaire to their clients. The questionnaire format has the advantages of being impersonal, and helping the client to pinpoint their areas of concern without being intrusive.

- *By using an external consultant* Clients may discuss the reasons for the failure of a proposal more readily with a disinterested third party than they will with those personally involved. If knowing the reasons for failure is vitally important to you, and the client is willing to take the time, the investment in an hour or two of a consultant's time may be well worthwhile.

Sadly, you may never know what went wrong. Sometimes, factors other than the proposal may have been at work – for example, the client may just have been trying to 'gee up' their existing supplier by introducing a little competition. But it is always worth asking – the answers may be painful, but they will undoubtedly help you to improve your performance.

Internal follow-up

Every proposal, whether successful or unsuccessful, provides a learning opportunity that should not be wasted. Always organize follow-up meetings on your proposals. Involve both the proposal team and other members of the company who might have something to contribute. Look at issues such as:

- What did the client have to say about the proposal?
- Did your ideas meet the need?
- Was the proposal written to bring out the benefits to the client?
- Did successful proposals use any new ideas in terms of content or presentation that could be applied to future proposals?
- Did you field the right team:
  – for the proposed project?
  – for the presentation?
- Was the price right?

Record the key points that come out of follow-up meetings and store them with the proposal on your proposal database. It's important to be aware that, following an unsuccessful proposal, people will be feeling sensitive. An open, constructive approach is vital.

Summary

- Wherever possible, ask the client for the reasons why your proposal was successful or unsuccessful.

- Make internal follow-up meetings part of your routine.

- Record the results of follow-up in your proposal database.

Action points

1   If you are not yet in the habit of asking the client about the reasons for success or failure, start with your next proposal.

2   Put together a checklist that you can use to guide internal follow-up, and which can be conveniently entered on your proposal database.

3   Conduct a three-monthly or six-monthly review of your successful and unsuccessful proposals. What features did the successful ones have in common?

Further reading

Buzan, T., *The mind map book*, BBC Books, 1993.

Cooper, B.M., *Writing technical reports*, Pelican, 1964 (still in print).

De Bono, E., *Serious creativity*, HarperCollins, 1992.

The Economist pocket style book, Economist Publications, 1987.

Fowler, H.W., *Fowler's modern English usage*, Oxford University Press, 1965.

Gowers, E., *The complete plain words*, Pelican, 1973.

Janner, G., *Janner on pitching for business*, Hutchinson Business Books, 1990.

Minto, B., *The pyramid principle. Logic in writing and thinking*, Pitman, 1987.

Partridge, E., *Usage and abusage. A guide to good English*, Hamish Hamilton, 1965.

Strunk, W. and White, E.B., *The elements of style*, Macmillan, 1979 (still in print).

Index